Eddie Piorek

Forward by Carol Wimber

"Dedicated to all the pioneers of early Vineyard"

"Many thanks to Michele, Janet and Noah for their aesthetic contributions. And to Carol, Carl and Randy for their insightful interviews."

TABLE OF CONTENTS

Forward 1

Introduction. 3

Chapter 1 "MERCY" 7

Chapter 2 "WORSHIP" 15

Chapter 3 "BASILEIA" 23

Chapter 4 "LONNIE" 31

Chapter 5 "HEALING". 37

Chapter 6 "DELIVERANCE". 43

Chapter 7 "MORRO BAY" 53

Chapter 8 "McCLURE". 57

PHOTOS 64

Chapter 9 "CHEERS" 73

Chapter 10 "THE PROPHETIC" 81

Chapter 11 "THE FATHER'S LOVE" 91

Chapter 12 "POWER EVANGELISM". 99

Chapter 13 "INNER HEALING" 107

Chapter 14 "BIG TACO" 115

Chapter 15 "RENEWAL" 121

Chapter 16 'MINISTRY TEAM". 129

Chapter 17 "WAITING ON THE SPIRIT" 139

Chapter 18 "WIMBERISMS" 147

Epilogue. 155

FORWARD
By Carol Wimber

There are many reasons that I could list concerning why I am so very pleased that Eddie has written this book but it's probable the main reason is simply: I love the man! I love the way he thinks. I love his courage and determination to live out what the Lord has anointed him to do. I love him like I love my sons. So did John...from the first day he met him. We loved Eddie and Jan as if they were ours. I really can't explain it. One of those things I guess. John and I would discuss it sometimes but always left it at "Don't understand it all but I love those kids! They give me pleasure... the way they go after God! They are both All-In...not holding anything back. Wish I had a hundred of 'em!".

Eddie delighted in the things of God, the treasures of His Holy Spirit. He still does! He's still the same! A fearless disciple...well, at the beginning, if not always fearless, then Brave is the word! He never let that fear stop him from going into the deep water. An eager and steadfast disciple of Jesus and his Holy Spirit. As time went on the Father himself revealed His Love to Eddie and through Eddie. Powerful stuff!

John and I always knew that if Eddie was there at the conference or church or whatever venue he would teach from, the Holy Spirit would have his way with the people. We knew for sure that the Lord would manifest Himself there. In fact, although it's a whole different story, I had to stop him from raising John from the dead! I had no doubt that he would and that he could but I had promised John that we would let him go home. All the way home where he longed to be. "Don't do it Eddie! I promised him!" when he laid his hand on John's poor brain-dead head and the dials and monitors started jumping around.

At one point in the Vineyard when outside influences had, in my opinion, sort of warped what I believe to be our marching orders from God. In my memory I have this scene. I had entered the church auditorium to see that Eddie was about to speak. He was just standing there as the couple thousand people found their seats. He was just standing there in the stage. No notes, no music, no introduction, just him holding a soft drink can in his hand. It got very quiet in that way that happens when the Lord is about to say something. "Classic Coke" he explained holding the can up and quietly and with power he went on to remind the Vineyard of our call, our marching orders, our Classic Vineyard. Unforgettable time.

When I read this wonderful, amazing little book it made me cry. In every chapter I was taken back to our simple, childlike, holy, unpretentious, joyful beginnings. Thank you Eddie, for writing it down. - Carol Wimber

INTRODUCTION

Pop! Fizz! Effervescence waft in the air.

As was my practice I had just pulled the pop-top off an ice cold Coke in order to take a swig before I started my sermon.

I was in Germany, standing before a young audience that comprised the Vineyard in Munich. The pastor had asked me to share about the values and practices of the early Vineyard. John Wimber had recently passed away and the pastor knew that I had spent a lot of time with him. Seventeen years to be exact.

As I was gathering my thoughts to speak I was drawn to look at the red and white can I was holding. In big swirling script the logo jumped out to me - Classic Coke! The title of my message was born: Classic Vineyard.

Perusing the label, my introductory description of Classic Vineyard was illuminated. "Always refreshing" - the manifest presence of the Spirit flowed through everything we did. "Original Formula" - there was always the primary mix of worship, the Word and doing the works. Always.

I think John Wimber captured an amazingly logical flow in identifying these three crucial original ingredients. It was in worship that this intimacy in the presence of God was discovered. And once this immediate presence was in the room there needed to be an appropriate explanation in the Word of God. The biblical explanation was that the kingdom of God was in our midst. With that he preached the Gospel of the kingdom. Now if you preach that you have climbed out on a bit of a limb. If the kingdom is in our midst then we must do the works of the kingdom. Like Jesus, we must heal the sick, cast out demons and perchance, even raise the dead.

Whoa! This sequence is a paradigm shifter. With this flow John enacted a unique blend of Evangelical theology and Pentecostal experience. And he became a credible, and may I add, incredible, witness for me and many others to follow. Wherever I travel around the world I hear testimonies in so many different streams of ministry of how John's life and message influenced their kingdom journey.

In the year following John's passing, I had the opportunity to preach at the New Beginnings Conference at the Anaheim Vineyard. I began by pulling the top off another can of Classic Coke. There was the familiar "Pop! Fizz!" I then articulated the "original formula" for Classic Vineyard. That night the presence was manifest afresh in worship, the Word and the works of the kingdom. The video recorded that night was seen around the world.

And so, Classic Vineyard is the title for this little book. It is not a comprehensive history of the Vineyard nor an apologetic for it's theology. It is simply a collection of personal stories about the early days of the Vineyard focusing on hanging out with John, listening to his remarkable teaching and embarking on the radical adventure of "doing the stuff" together. It is written as a reminder of our rich spiritual heritage with the hope of renewing our resolve as we press on into the kingdom coming today.

"Pop! Fizz!" Let's begin.

1

MERCY

Mercy is often born in a moment. Like the one in Victor Hugo's Les Miserables, when Jean Valjean was caught with the stolen silverware and the fatherly Monsignor Bienvenu told the police that they were a gift from him. Valjean, previously imprisoned for twenty years for stealing a loaf of bread when starving had known only judgement for life's failures. Mercy was born with the silverware and grace swiftly followed when the Monsignor added, "But you forgot the candlesticks!"

In 1981, the moment of mercy's epiphany occurred for my wife Janet and I, not in a French monastery, but in a Charlie Brown's restaurant in Anaheim, California. John and Carol Wimber had invited us to join them, along with Blaine and Becky Cook, for a meal after a Sunday night service at Canyon High School. Charlie Brown's was a nice steak house and a bit pricier than Janet and I were accustomed. Knowing that we had only twenty-five dollars on us we quietly agreed to order moderately. But John had other ideas.

First, he ordered appetizers for all. Then he insisted that we all enjoy the fine and "expensive" steaks. As Janet and I chewed, and smiled outwardly, inwardly our stomachs churned with anxiety as we silently calculated what our fair share would be. By the time dessert was over we realized we were in big trouble. The moment of truth came when the waiter placed the check on the table. Doom hung in the air. Then suddenly a pudgy, freckled hand whisked it away. And with a smile John looked at us and said, "I've got it." And in that moment mercy was born in us.

Mercy was exactly what Janet and I were in great need of at the time. We were in the process of recovering from a recent traumatic church experience. After years of dedicated service I had lost my pastoral staff position, forcing us to leave our beloved church community. The crisis began, when out of personal need, I hungered for a more powerful experience of the Spirit's power. Upon suggesting to our elder board my desire to lead the church in that direction I ran into a serious questioning of my leadership abilities, not to mention my mental faculties. I was asked to take a leave of absence while they assessed the situation. A time of judgment began.

Several weeks before the crisis I had attended a conference where John Wimber was teaching on evangelism. In it, he made a passing comment about laying hands on burned-out pastors and seeing them freshly empowered by the Spirit. Something deep inside me told me that was exactly what I needed. So when things began to go seriously wrong in our negotiations with our elders, Janet encouraged me to get some counsel from that John "Wembley" guy. Perhaps he could help me. As usual she was right and so I made an appointment to see him.

After waiting several weeks John returned from an overseas conference. I met with him at the old Wagner House office in Yorba Linda. I was expecting him to tell me that I just didn't have what it takes to lead the church. I was expecting further judgement. Instead he explained the dysfunction of the type of church government I was under and that I was probably the true pastor. He laid hands on me, prayed and then prophesied about my pastoral calling. I felt the manifest winds of the Spirit powerfully blowing off the dust of my original calling. It was the first breath of mercy into my gasping soul. With renewed enthusiasm I returned and presented an appeal to the elders to lead the congregation into more of the Spirit. The immediate result was six weeks severance. Shell-shocked and staggering under a sense of failure, Janet and I limped into Canyon High on Sunday nights. Fortunately we were on the path to being found by mercy.

Mercy visited us week after week as we attended the evening services. On our very first visit we experienced it as a palpable feeling without knowing what name to put on it. Sitting high up in the gymnasium bleachers we had a good view of the stage. The band reminded me of the Hippyrock groups that led worship at the tent revivals in the Jesus Movement. But with the first note I knew something was different. The sound was softer and intensely intimate. Listening to lyrics like "Let the Son of God enfold you with His Spirit and His love…" tears would well up within me. As worship continued on I found myself openly weeping as the presence of God descended upon me. In the nights that followed, John's teaching gave a name to this heartwarming presence. Mercy.

In the months that followed Janet and I brought up a small rag-tag group of new church planters from San Clemente to glean from the Canyon High meetings. During one of those meetings something occurred that birthed a new perspective on mercy in my life and ministry.

A woman named Susan, who had an urgent need for healing, came with us. Weeks earlier, after suffering a sore throat for several days, she went to the hospital emergency room. While there, her trouble breathing increased sharply. Suddenly her epiglottis (the cartilage at the base of the tongue) swelled shut. An emergency tracheotomy was performed that saved her life. Several weeks later the swelling remained and the trachea tube looked to be a permanent fixture. It was still in place when we we went to the back-room for prayer.

The ministry team prayed for her for some time with no visible results. As they continued I had these thoughts going through my mind, "I think I know why she has this condition and is not getting better. She, a divorcee, is currently having an affair with a married man." In other words, I believed her affliction and lack of healing was a judgement from God.

Hoping to bring light to the situation, I took the man leading the prayer team aside and whispered in his ear what I thought was going on. The man, Jack Sims, looked at me and said, "Eddie, I think God intends to teach you something about His mercy through this situation." Then he went back to praying for Susan without bringing up anything I mentioned. You could see by her tears that Susan was being deeply touched but the condition and the trachea tube remained. The team encouraged us to keep regularly praying for her upon our return home. And that we did.

About one week later, Janet and I received a phone call early in the morning. On the other end was a joyfully weeping Susan. She told us how she went to bed as usual with the tube in place. When she woke up in the morning she was amazed to see the breathing tube sitting upright on her bed stand. When she felt her throat and the wound was closed she was absolutely astounded! She was breathing freely again! She was completely healed. Today, over thirty years later, she recounts, "I was in an adulterous relationship. Sin separates us from God. Why was I spared death? Lavish mercy? Yes!!!"

When John heard of this miracle he asked Susan to share on a Sunday night. After she shared her moving testimony, I read this Bible text where Jesus answers the Pharisees who are questioning his eating with tax collectors and sinners:

"On hearing this, Jesus said, "It is not the healthy who need a doctor, but the sick. But go and learn what this means: 'I desire mercy, not sacrifice.' For I have not come to call the righteous, but sinners." (Matthew 9:12-13)

I went on to share how I was learning big lessons in the school of mercy. We were all enrolled in mercy classes. Even John shared of his learning curve. He often told a story of praying for a sick woman without much faith that she would be healed. But nevertheless she was! On returning home after her healing he had this vision:

"Suddenly in my minds eye there appeared to be a cloud bank superimposed across the sky. But I had never seen a cloud bank like this one, so I pulled the car over to the side of the road to take a closer look. Then I realized it was not a cloud bank; it was a honeycomb with honey dripping out on the people below…I was awestruck. Not knowing what to think I prayed, "Lord, what is it?" He said. "It's my mercy, John…There's plenty for everyone…"

That vision of mercy had a powerful effect on John. Mercy permeated everything he did, especially his teaching. One of my favorite's was when he preached on Blind Bartimaeus (Like 18:35-43). With great drama he echoed Bartimaeus' cry, "Jesus, Son of David, have mercy on me!" With even greater dramatics he echoed "Bart's" response to Jesus' question, "What do you want me to do for you?" With his stocky finger pointing to his eye John shouted out, "Lord, I want to see!" And see he did.

Some thirty-four years later I realize that the these lessons in the school of mercy have stuck with me. My favorite prayer these days is the Jesus Prayer, "Lord Jesus Christ, have mercy on me!" I pray it dozens of time each day on many occasions and in differing situations. It's a prayer that always receives a swift answer.

Sometimes I even get to pray it over someone else. Like the other day when I stopped by a local donut shop and noticed one of my regular servers, Anita, was absent. Anita was an Hispanic single mother of four who had been abandoned by her abusive husband. She struggled with a deep sense of failure and self-condemnation. She worked back to back day jobs and struggled to make ends meet. Upon asking where Anita was I was told she was in the kitchen and not feeling well.

When I stuck my head through the kitchen door I saw her bent over in pain. She had a greatly swollen abdomen due to a severe kidney infection. She was crying and was so worried about missing work and losing her job. I felt a surge of compassion and tears welled up in my eyes. Given her permission and only a moment to pray for her, I chose the best one-line prayer I knew, "Lord Jesus have mercy on Anita." She wept and said she felt a little better.

Upon returning the next day she was back out front serving customers with a big smile. I could see her swollen condition was gone. She told me that all the pain and swelling disappeared overnight. I asked her if she realized who healed her? She immediately answered, "Jesus!" "Correct!", I said, and then asked her if she wanted to receive the One who healed her to live in her heart. She said, "Oh, yes!" I led her in a simple prayer, "Lord Jesus have mercy on me." And He did! Several weeks later she invited my wife and I over for dinner. She had left the donut shop, started her own business making tamales and was doing quite well for herself. Mercy made the difference.

A younger Vineyard pastor recently asked me what I thought the core values of the Vineyard were. The first one that came to my mind was mercy. You might say it is the prime paradigm shift that occurs in Vineyard spirituality. Faith in a merciful God frees us from the tyranny of religious performance lived under the fear of failure and impending judgment. Manifest mercy activates forgiveness for sin freeing us from condemnation. Mercy catalyses a compassionate heart that really cares for others. Mercy connects us to the heart of worship: intimacy with a loving God. Mercy becomes the interpretive key for the Word of God. Mercy can't help but empower kingdom works to break out in our world. Mercy just may be the currency of the kingdom.

2

WORSHIP

Last Sunday we visited the Anaheim Vineyard. As worship began I lifted my eyes towards the musicians on stage, then to the ceiling high above, took a deep breath, and said to myself, "This is a good place to worship! In the house that John built." Then some familiar chords were struck and these words flashed on the screen:

Oh Lord, have mercy on me, and heal me,
Oh Lord, have mercy on me, and free me,
Place my feet upon a rock,
Put a new song in my heart, in my heart,
Oh Lord, have mercy on me.
(Carl Tuttle)[1]

My heart skipped a beat, my mouth formed the words automatically and I was transported back to the early days at Canyon High School. Those leading the worship were John Wimber, Eddie Espinoza and Carl Tuttle.

Carl recently told me that the most amazing thing about worship in the gym was the "weight of the presence" that could be felt. The pursuit of that presence of Jesus birthed extended worship with sets of 12-17 songs. The songs were kept simple, learned without song sheets or overheads. The lyrics were intimate and targeted to touch the heart of Jesus.

Consider how He loves you
His arms of love enfold you
Like a sweet, sweet perfume
Your prayers are very precious
They reach the heart of Jesus
Like a sweet, sweet perfume
(Carol Wimber)[2]

I have always loved to worship, from singing classic hymns in the Presbyterian Church with the aid of a choir, to hand-clapping to Catholic Charismatic folksongs which were cutting edge in the 70's, to swaying to "Come to the Waters" at Calvary Chapel during the Jesus Movement. The thing that I always liked best was the sense of entering into a heavenly realm for a moment. The realm of the manifest presence of God. But those moments seem short-lived as we were on to teaching and preaching. In Canyon High School the moment was protracted long enough that worship began to re-define itself. It seemed to become the reason for being there. Carol Wimber's perspective:

"Jesus gives us everything. Everything. Everything is for us. The Worship is for Him! Only for Him. It's our part... what we do for Him. Everything else He does for us...So we WORSHIP HIM."

This worship was contagious and we wanted to take it home with us. John Wimber, realizing the need to make it transferrable, leaned over to Carl Tuttle during one service and said, "Carl, you need to develop a theology of worship!" Carl gathered some friends to look up all the references to worship in the Bible and write them on 3 x 5 cards. Turns out there were around 600. From there he synthesized it down to what became a worship seminar. I, like many other hungry pastors, had Carl come and teach it in our churches.

Worship spread as new songs were written capturing this unique essence of intimacy. Carol Wimber, reminding songwriters of how important their gift was said, " When the sermons are long forgotten we will remember the songs the Holy Spirit gives us." So true! Whenever a song like "Isn't He" begins, we all close our eyes and sing. No need for the aid of a projection screen. Our hearts remember every word.

Vineyard worship exploded as new songs were written, recorded and published though Mercy Records. In 1985, John hired Randy Rigby to develop this new entity. The first album, "Just Like You Promised" was recorded in Costa Mesa, California. Randy's perspective: "John Wimber was very pleased with the outcome and he didn't fire me...

hahaha! While at the studio and sitting at the recording console reviewing the mixes, he pulled down his glasses and gave me a very intense look and said, 'I've heard music before and this sounds just like it.' We recorded and published a lot more songs after that."

Thinking of Randy provides a good segue to sharing about developing worship in our local church. It was so easy to worship in the atmosphere at Canyon High with the excellent musicianship there. It was not so easy to find musicians of that caliber back home, however, one saving element was that our people loved to worship so much they overlooked the occasional missed note. And apparently so did the Holy Spirit because he always showed up and filled us with his lovely presence.

When Randy came, things dramatically improved in our worship. While attending our Father's Day picnic Randy bared his neanderthal chest and handily won our hairy man contest and a gift set of my Father Loves You cassettes. The Father's love won him over and he joined our community. After several Sundays of observing our one male guitarist and one female vocalist lead worship he asked if he could be of some assistance. The next week he was on stage backing them up with his superb keyboards.

Then one afternoon he came by the church office and asked if he could introduce some friends. They had just moved down from Los Osos. They, along with their four kids, were camped out in a station wagon, parked in Randy's driveway. They were seeking the Lord's direction. When I agreed to pray for them he brought them into my tiny office and sat them down on the couch across from me. Their names were John and Marie Barnett.

I had never heard of them. But when I began to pray I felt the Spirit quicken me and I began to prophecy about them having a worship ministry, writing songs that would circle the earth. I went on and on. It was a really "big prophecy". When it was over I was embarrassed. What had I done? After all, I knew nothing about them. Perhaps they thought I was out of my mind. However I saw tears in their eyes and sensed a quiet agreement in their hearts. Well, history has spoken concerning the validity of that word.

John and Marie were our worship leaders for ten years at Mission Viejo Vineyard. John and I were the proverbial "odd couple." I wore Nordstrom slacks, Ralph Lauren shirts and Cole Hahn loafers. John wore blue jeans, flannel shirts, work boots and sometimes, a knit stocking cap, even during the Summer. When I would suggest incorporating songs by other writers, he'd often give me a frowned look and then play his own, often for an extended period of time. But we really grew to love each other and I learned so much about authenticity and passion in worship from he and Marie.

They never missed a Sunday morning or evening. Incredible faithfulness. And the new songs…amazing. Especially the ones capturing the revelation of the Father's love:

"Father of Lights", "Unending Love" and "Redeemed." Each one helping us to worship the Father and experience his love. We had many adventures taking this message and music throughout the United States, Canada and New Zealand.

John never failed to represent classic vineyard worship with its simplicity and pursuit of intimacy. I remember teaching a seminar on the Father's love in Kansas City with over 2500 in attendance. The demographic of the attendees was more pentecostal and the worship team of a dozen on stage were pretty fervent in their style of praise. The audience was "fired up" when I was introduced to speak. Needing to "dial things down" a bit, and compose myself, I invited John to come up and lead us in a song. I'll never forget John standing alone on stage and taking out a piece of crumpled paper to sing a song that he had written that morning, "Who Would Not love You." He began to strum the melody on his acoustic guitar and sing the song as if no one was there except he and the Father. The Spirit came and there was not a dry eye in the house.

Several years later our church met for our Sunday night service. It was a smaller group, under a hundred. You know, the faithful ones who just love to worship. That night, John and Marie were on stage leading us. Simple songs. The Spirit of the Lord brooding over us. And then Marie began to sing. Spontaneously. Something prophetic. We just listened as the words formed:

This is the air I breathe
This is the air I breathe
Your holy presence
Living in me [3]

And you know the rest.

For the last seven years Janet and I have opened our home on Tuesday nights to invite people into that timeless presence. The first thing we do is worship. It is usually the best thing we do. Things have not really changed much. Chris Lizotte, one of our current worship leaders, was there in Canyon High School. He captures his experience of the essence of worship both then and now.

"Worship music in the 80s back at the Canyon High Gym was a new experience for me. I had never felt that way while songs were being sung in a gym filled with people. It was a great experience knowing the presence of the Holy Spirit was tangible. Now as I'm older and still learning and experiencing the Holy Spirit in new ways, I'm finding that worship is offered in many different forms. Like praising God along with the songs of creation, and just being still and knowing He is God. These things and more, are truths I've been learning through our Tuesday night fellowship at Eddie and Janet's. They're helping this worship leader learn how to listen and join in. Whether in silence, or in the sounds of voices and instruments, or in the sounds of life. It's all Worship."

Amen!

Footnotes:
1. Permission granted by Carl Tuttle.
2. Permission granted by Carol Wimber.
3. Written by Marie Barnett.
CCLI#1874117 ©1995 Mercy/Vineyard Publishing (ASCAP).
All Rights Reserved. International Copyright Secured.
Used By Permission.

3

BASILEIA

Basileia, pronounced "bas-il-i'-ah, is the word that puts the "kapow" in the kingdom of God. John Wimber defines it as such:

"In the New Testament, the Greek word basileia means 'kingship' or 'royal rule'. It is normally translated 'kingdom'. It implies exercise of kingly rule or reign rather than simply a geographic realm over which a king rules...the biblical concept goes beyond the idea of realm to emphasize a dynamic rule."[1]

God rules where his love and power are manifest. Of course that love and power is perfectly manifest in heaven and someday we will go there and really enjoy it! But this rule is also manifest wherever heaven's rule comes to earth by the power of the Holy Spirit. It's then we feel the "kapow" of the kingdom.

For the first fourteen years of my christian life when I thought of the kingdom of God, I thought primarily about the future. The focus of my ministry was getting people saved and ready for heaven. And that's not a bad focus. Salvation is often a "kapow" experience.

In those days, my wife and I operated a Bible-bookstore and Hal Lindsey's Late Great Planet Earth was our bestseller. As a lay youth minister, I preached Hal's take on the End Times, the Rapture and the Tribulation, leading many teenagers to avoid the mark of the Beast by receiving Jesus as their Savior. Not a bad result. My wife still reminds me that many of them are in the ministry today.

Along with this future focus, I developed a very conservative position on the way the Holy Spirit moved today. The Spirit's powerful in-breaking into our "here and now" with gifts, healing, deliverances, etc. was not on my radar. I was as buttoned-down on the things of the Spirit as the blue oxford shirt and tie that I wore when I preached.

Once, back then, we had dinner with a couple visiting our church. He was a seminary graduate. She was a lovely lady who happened to be suffering with cancer. He made a casual comment about his observations of our church. Quoting Jesus, from Matthew 6:33, "Seek first the kingdom of God and his righteousness and all these things will be added unto you." he said that we were certainly a congregation seeking to live righteously according to the Word of God. And then added, "But what about seeking the kingdom of God, the powerful rule of God here on earth. My wife needs the power of that kingdom." His new definition of the kingdom sent a fracture line though my conservative doctrine.

Experience has a way of dismantling our dogma. Mine was changed when our church split, resulting in a personal crisis in my self-confidence, and a counseling appointment with John Wimber. After analyzing my situation, John laid his hand on my head, and prayed for me, and "kapow", I felt something like a mighty rushing wind pass through me, body and soul. A seismic shift took place within my thinking about the kingdom of God.

That shift led me to plant a Calvary Chapel Church, under the tutoring of Chuck Smith Jr. In the process I attended a leaders training class at his church. Looking back, I realize now that I had a critical need to learn new theological language for my recent experience in the Holy Spirit. That language was found in our textbook, George Eldon Ladd's, A Theology of the New Testament. Here's an excerpt:

"There is a two-fold dualism in the New Testament: God's will is done in heaven; his kingdom brings it to earth. In the Age to Come, heaven descends to earth and lifts historical existence to a new level of redeemed life."[2]

Ah! The kingdom of God has two dimensions; a "now" aspect and a "not yet" aspect. My theological background focused almost entirely on looking towards the "not yet" aspect of the kingdom. My experience in John's office of heaven's power breaking into my life was a good example of the "now" aspect of the kingdom. Ladd's teaching not only helped me to appreciate both dimensions of the kingdom but better understand the ministry of Jesus.

When Jesus said, "The time has come…The kingdom of God has come. Repent and believe the good news!" (Mark 1:15) he was announcing the basiliea, the rule of heaven coming to earth. The King had come to earth to make things right. To make them like they were in heaven. He came preaching the "word" of the kingdom and doing the "works" of the kingdom. He was putting the "kapow" back in kingdom of God.

Jesus went throughout Galilee, teaching in their synagogues, proclaiming the good news of the kingdom, and healing every disease and sickness among the people. 24 News about him spread all over Syria, and people brought to him all who were ill with various diseases, those suffering severe pain, the demon-possessed, those having seizures, and the paralyzed; and he healed them. (Matthew 4:23-24)

As the "in-breaking" rule of God spread, Jesus commissioned his disciples to the "word and work-force."
As you go, proclaim this message: 'The kingdom of heaven has come near.' 8 Heal the sick, raise the dead, cleanse those who have leprosy, drive out demons. Freely you have received; freely give. (Matthew 10:5-8)

These "Word-workers" were powerfully multiplied through John Wimber's ministry. Through his MC510 class at Fuller Seminary, his Signs and Wonders Conferences and Healing Seminars, a precise foundation of kingdom theology was laid. A powerful demonstration of kingdom works followed.

There is nothing quite like a miracle to convince you of the basileia of God. In 1985, I was in England preaching on Luke 12:32: "Do not be afraid, little flock, for your Father has been pleased to give you the kingdom." After telling the people that the Father loved them, liked them, and would be pleased to give them the kingdom, I invited them to come forward for prayer. Immediately an elderly woman rushed to the front with her head bowed down. As I asked her what she wanted from the Father, she looked up and pointing to a milky white eye she said, "I want my sight!" Unnerved by her boldness I placed my shaking hand over her eye and began my best prayer. Before I finished the first sentence she cried out, "I can see!" Her eye was completely clear. Yes, the Father loves to give us the basileia.

Probably the most dramatic demonstration of the reality of God's rule is seen in deliverance. Jesus said, "But if I drive out demons by the finger of God then the kingdom of God has come to you." (Luke 11:20). Talk about the "ka-pow" of the kingdom. Many times I proclaimed this verse over crowds of people in my workshops on deliverance all over the world. The result was always the same - all Hell broke loose!

But I am beginning to realize that this in-breaking rule of God is much bigger, more permeating and multifaceted than I first realized. It is more than just "signs and wonders." Once while having lunch with Ken Blue, a well educated friend, we were discussing how the "kingdom comes" in contemplative prayer. There the focus is on the indwelling presence of God versus the powerful in-breaking as seen in signs and wonders. He made a very insightful statement, "It's all kingdom!". All activity that restores the rule of heaven on earth is kingdom activity.

Over the years many Vineyards have expanded basileia to feeding the poor, recovery programs for addiction and justice ministry for victims of human trafficking. Even ecological awareness and care for the planet are part of the great restoration. Art and music join in the announcement of God's loving re-creativity at work. N. T. Wright says it well: "But how can the church announce that God is God, that Jesus is Lord, that the powers of evil, corruption, and death itself have been defeated, and that God's new world has begun? - if it's actively involved in seeking justice in the world, both globally and locally, and if it's cheerily celebrating God's good creation and its rescue from corruption in art and music, and if, in addition, its own internal life gives every sign that new creation is indeed happening, generating a new type of community - then suddenly the announcement makes a lot of sense."[3]

Yes, the basileia is probably bigger and better than we first realized. While it is good to forge ahead in all of its dimensions, it is wise not to forget that it all began with signs and wonders. It began with the coming of the King himself to plant the flag of his rule in the soil of planet earth with signs and wonders following. And following Jesus means not taking our hands off the plow of the kingdom. It means to keep on, as John used to put it, "Doing the stuff!" No matter what.

This last February, 2016, I ministered to a group of leaders at the Vineyard in Arroyo Grande, California. I had a prophetic word for the meeting: "Reuppance." Now I know that it's not a real word but it's a take on "re-upping", like a soldier does for another term of service somewhere. The spiritual application being that from time to time we, as Christian soldiers, need to re-up again for the kingdom, for the "basileia," to actively bring heaven's rule to earth.

In reminding those leaders, my teaching reminded me of my own need to "re-up". I did so by preaching the next day, Sunday, on the power of the Gospel. When I finished, I pulled out a list of words of knowledge the Spirit gave me for that morning. I read the list and people came forward. As we prayed for them the "basileia" came. A few experienced a loving "kapow!"

Footnotes
1. John Wimber, Power Evangelism (Chosen, 2014), p. 33.
2. George Eldon Ladd, A Theology of the New Testament (Eerdmans, 1974), p. 69.
3. N.T. Wright, Surprised by Hope (Harper One, 2008), p. 227-8.

4

LONNIE

The pews of Maranatha Chapel were packed and eyes glistened with tears, as Love Song finished their worship set. Pastor Chuck (Smith) sat on his stool, opened the Bible and began to teach. When he was finished, he invited everyone to stay for the "afterglow", a time of prolonged ministry of the Holy Spirit. A long-haired, bearded, and barefoot, "hippie-looking" young man by the name of Lonnie Frisbee led that particular ministry time. My wife and I had heard rumors of the wild things that occurred there. Such things as speaking in tongues, swooning in the Spirit and supernatural healing. We loved the music and teaching on those Monday night meetings in the early days of the Jesus Movement. However, as conservative Evangelicals, we "chickened out" of attending the afterglow.

Thirteen years later there was no "chickening out". We were part of a ministry team that had traveled to Staten Island with John Wimber for a healing conference. The same Lonnie Frisbee was slated to lead the ministry time there…

the "afterglow." It turned out to be a night to remember. There were several hundred in the sanctuary of the Pentecostal church. The worship was lively, loud and upbeat to say the least. If anything could persuade God to show up it would have been that worship. Then the pastor got up and introduced John as a great "signs and wonders-worker." The audience was on the edge of their seats with anticipation of the Spirit's powerful coming.

John, wearing the only pair of faded blue-jeans I saw in the place, meandered up onto the stage and positioned himself behind the keyboard. He began to play softly one of his intimate worship songs. Everyone began to relax as the Spirit flowed gently through the congregation. When John finished, he said, "Ah, can't you feel His presence. He has been here all along." From that quiet place John began to preach on the healing ministry of Jesus. When he was through he introduced Lonnie.

Lonnie shared for a few minutes on how the church had grieved the Holy Spirit but "He was over it now" and would come again by invitation. He asked everyone to stand. He then prayed a simple prayer, "Come Holy Spirit!" I was standing at the end of the front row, perfectly positioned to observe what happened next. It was as though a gale force wind hit those in the front row. An unseen hand sent them bouncing like bowling pins into the row behind them. And those into the row behind them. Like fish cast up on the sand after a surging wave dozens of people lay shaking in the

Spirit. That's when the ministry team went to work praying for people to be saved, delivered and healed. I would see this kind of raw power again in South Africa, but never again since.

After the conference the team gathered at a famous Italian restaurant on Coney Island called Carolinas. Our New York brethren, Mike and Char Turrigiano and Randy and Pat Larson, knew it well. But Lonnie was the master of ceremonies. Upon our arrival he ordered wine and the best baked clams in the world. We wined and dined for hours. All of us sharing stories from the ministry times. Lonnie always had the best stories. So much laughter and Holy Spirit joy. Such a baptism of freedom for my wife and I after some very legalistic years. I realize that some, including Lonnie, would struggle with finding boundaries for their freedom in the years to come. But in the beginning it was pure celebration.

In 1982, Janet and I joined a Vineyard team of eighty traveling to Johannesburg, South Africa. Our goal was to plant the first Vineyard church on the continent. We all stayed in the same "two-star," high rise hotel, in what is now the dangerous Hillbrow district. That's where we got to know Lonnie better. Once at dinner we were all presented with ox-tail soup. Some of the tail-bones still had a little fur on them. During the meal I noticed that Lonnie had fished out the circular bones and fit them together on his plate. They took the perfect shape of the ox's tail. Looking up at us he said, "Excuse me, but I am not eating the tail of anything."

In the meetings we saw more of the power side of Lonnie's ministry. Like the time when he had everyone under twenty-five stand, and ring the perimeter walls of the gymnasium where the conference was being held. He then proceeded to invite the Holy Spirit to come as he pantomimed shooting them with a pistol. Not a young man or woman was left standing. All fell, or might I say were thrown down to the floor. Some cried out to be saved, others violently shook as demons fled, and others wept as cancers were cleansed from bodies. The public, raw power side of Lonnie Frisbee. Awesome!

Days later the team travelled to an elegant retreat center some distance from Johannesburg. It was surrounded by an African game park. Lonnie, who had been there before, became our tour guide. With Jack Hanna enthusiasm, he pointed out the giraffes whose necks rose up from the eucalyptus trees off in the distance. He authoritatively warned us to roll up the windows of our combi-van as we passed a pride of lions feeding on a slain antelope.

Upon returning to the center the team had a lunch with the local South African pastors. After John led a question and answer session about the conference and the newly formed Vineyard, he asked Lonnie to pray for the pastors. Lonnie again invited the Holy Spirit to come. And come He did! After Lonnie spoke a prophetic word over one man, he fell backwards to the ground, lay there for a moment, and then was launched horizontally nearly four feet in the air. A move, in my estimation, humanly impossible to perform.

Flopping like a fish, his heels flared out nearly kicking us, and Lonnie.

In the midst of the encounter as we were all focused on the man, Lonnie slipped to the side, put his hands on his knees and looked dazed. He was actually frightened by the violence of the phenomenon. On the bus ride back to the hotel I sat next to him. He looked at me and said, "Did I do something wrong?" He turned his face to the window and gazed at the African countryside. He was crying. For the first time I saw the fearful child within him. The private, pained side of Lonnie Frisbee. I felt compassion for him.

The next year Lonnie traveled down to San Clemente and ministered at our Sunday night service. As usual powerful things happened. One moment that I will never forget happened when he picked out my son Nathan, who was twelve at the time, and prophesied over him. He said, "The Spirit of the Lord is on the pastor's boy. You gave him to the Lord when he was born. The Lord gave him back to you, but tonight the Lord is taking him back." We had not introduced Nathan to Lonnie and he knew nothing about his near death at birth or our dedicating him to the Lord at that time. Of course, at the time, he had no idea that this prophesy would find fulfillment in Nathan's years of faithful service as a worship leader.

In the years that followed, reports of Lonnie's sexual struggles surfaced and the Vineyard leaders faced very difficult choices concerning his ministry. Attempts at counseling failed. He was seen less and less around the Vineyard. Focused on my own life and ministry I saw less of him myself. But I'll never forget the last time I saw him.

It was 1986 and I was preaching at the Anaheim Vineyard evening service. I had recently experienced the Father's love in my life and John had invited me to share about it. I had chosen the text in Romans 8 about the Spirit bringing us into the experience of Sonship; our adoption as God's children, causing us to cry out, "Abba, Father!" After the message, I invited the Holy Spirit to "come," just as I had seen Lonnie do so many times. The Spirit of Sonship fell in the room. Many began to receive the Father's love.

I invited those who wanted more to come forward for ministry…into the "afterglow." As I looked down from the stage at the crowd, it was as if the sea of humanity was parted, and one man stood alone, his head down. I felt led to go down to him. Putting my hand on his shoulder he looked up, his eyes glistening. It was Lonnie. I saw again the face of the frightened child that I first saw on the bus. He burst into tears, and threw his arms around me, exclaiming, "This is what I have been looking for my whole life! The Father's love!" I embraced him, wept with him and then blessed him with the Father's love. It was my last moment with Lonnie before he passed away years later.

I have never forgotten that moment or the many other precious and powerful moments with him. Thank you Lonnie for everything you gave to me, my family and to us in the Vineyard. Rest in Peace.

5

HEALING

As our plane began its descent into Phoenix I was asking the Father to show me what he would be doing in the healing conference John Wimber was leading there. I immediately had two words impressed upon my mind: detached retina. The next night as John began the ministry time he asked if anyone on the team had a "word" about someones need for healing. There were several. I remember Tom Stipe getting one about a brain tumor. I finally got up my courage and raised my hand. John asked me for my word. I said "I believe someone has a detached retina." He then asked, "Which eye?." On the spot, I spontaneously blurted out, "Right eye." In retrospect I guess I had a fifty-fifty chance of being right.

When John invited those responding to the words to come forward, people began to file down the aisles to the stage. The ministry team located the people who had the specific word for them and began to pray for them. After a while Tom and I were the only ones standing alone with no one responding. A lonely feeling. John asked one more time if anyone had the conditions mentioned. Then a man raised his hand and called out, "I have the tumor." I sensed Tom felt some relief as he welcomed the man up for prayer. I felt conspicuously alone. I was just about to go join the others in praying when I saw a man splitting the crowd making his way to the front. From a ways off I could see the scar on his right eye.

He was sixty years old and had been blind in that eye for forty years as result of an industrial accident where it was pierced by flying metal. After gaining this information we began our prayers waiting for precise directions from the Spirit. I was first led to ask him if he knew Jesus as his Savior? He said no but he would like to. We led him in a simple prayer for salvation. The presence of the Lord increased around him. I then asked him if he was fearful concerning his condition? He said he lived in fear of losing sight in his other eye. When we broke the power of his fear of blindness he was knocked back by the power of the Lord. Reaching down and holding him upright we began to address the healing of his eye. After several minutes we asked if there was any change. Blocking his good eye he reported seeing light and shadows for the first time through his damaged one. We continued on for some time until he could identify John standing on stage. Tears came to his eyes as well as ours. We all enjoyed a group hug with our hearts filled with joy.

Powerful healings like this were commonplace in the early Vineyard conferences. I imagine that the fact that they were cutting-edge kingdom events, filled with hundreds of faith-filled participants and not to mention John's sovereign anointing all contributed to that. However, another powerful factor was that we all got to participate in the healing process. John, contrary to many noted faith-healers, decentralized the prayer to ministry teams. He shared a user friendly model of prayer that worked not only on the conference stage but in our local churches and communities. Although often to a lesser degree we began to see healing upon our return home. We were "hooked on healing!"

Two year old Micah, suffering severe headaches and vomiting, was hospitalized for testing. As days passed without conclusive results, he lay in bed, in his mother's words, "like a zombie." Then I received a call from Blaine Cook. He said he had a word of knowledge concerning Micah's condition and would like to pray for him. Blaine believed he had viral encephalitis. Blaine came to the hospital and prayed for Micah. We all went home knowing Micah was in the Lord's hands. Here's what happened next in his mother's words: "The next day we returned to the hospital to find our son sitting up eating a hot dog and watching cartoons. He was totally healed. His probable diagnosis was viral encephalitis, the exact word Blaine had received."

One afternoon I had returned home from a long day at the office. Just as I was crashing on the couch there was a knock on the door. Opening it, I met my neighbor Jim who had a desperate look on his face. With tears in his eyes he urged me to come quickly and pray for his young daughter. She had excruciating pain in her knees and was about to leave for the doctors office. The day before they had done some blood tests and would now get the results back. Feeling exhausted and powerless I reluctantly went. When I saw the little girl in her pain my attitude changed. I laid my hand on her knee and asked Jesus to heal her. Immediately the pain left and never returned. At the doctors they confirmed the tests showed early onset rheumatoid arthritis. They were baffled by the absence of symptoms. Jim said, "I guess its not so bad to have a disease if you never have any symptoms."

In the following years we discovered that not all healings are "point of contact" healings like these were. Most required a process of time, technique and technology or in other words: sovereign providence, sustained prayer and professional medical help.

Steve Esslinger's healing was like this. He first came into my office with a diagnosis of advanced lymphoma with tumors pressing painfully against his vital organs. The doctors urged immediate heavy doses of chemotherapy, followed by surgery with the chances of success slim. He asked me what to do. I told him that everyone has to do what they felt was right for them, what they have faith for. He said he had faith to do nothing medically speaking. He had faith to trust in God alone.

For months Steve came forward for prayer at the end of Sunday services. Week after week the ministry team prayed for him. Each time he felt the fire of the Spirit touch his body causing him to get burning hot and sweat profusely. Several months later, the tumors were miraculously gone. For the next twenty years, Steve remained well, with only the help of some periodic Interferon treatments. He led an ultra-active life coaching sports, succeeding in business and helping non-profit organizations. His life inspired thousands. Then the cancer returned with a vengeance. Through radical prayer and state of the art technology Steve fought himself back to health. He went on to travel all around the world. And then, twenty-two years after the initial miracle, he had to fight it once more. This time Jesus mercifully took him home.

One of things I loved the most about John was how real and no nonsense he was. Especially in the area of healing. No hype, presumption or manipulation. In 1996, when John was not in the best of health himself I asked him if he could pray for my friend Tom. Tom had advanced prostrate cancer. His bones were riddled with large tumors. John said yes and invited us to meet him at a coffee shop in Yorba Linda. It was packed so we sat at the counter together. John and Tom got to know each other and then John said, "Tom, I am not getting a leading that you will be healed when I pray but you will get more time." Right there at the counter John reached over and laid hands on Tom praying, "Lord Jesus have mercy on Tom and bring him healing and more time. Tom lived supernaturally on that prayer for four more years.

Some thirty-four years after being commissioned by John into the kingdom ministry nothing is more mysterious to me than divine healing. Why are some healed and some not? Why this prayer or medicine works in one situation and not in another? Why the poor in third world situations are good candidates and affluent Westerners are sometimes not? Why some people have more anointing to heal than others? Even my best explanations don't fit every time. However, I have come to have no doubt that God is a merciful, healing God. No doubt that the power to heal is at work in the church. No doubt that everyone can "do the stuff" to some degree. No doubt that all are healed in the End. And to that end I will pray one more time for the next suffering person I meet. I know that's what John would do.

6

DELIVERANCE

It was approaching midnight, with winds howling and rain threatening, as I fumbled to fit the key into the darkened door of the little cottage that had been converted into our church office. Flipping the light on, my wife and I guided a young woman inside. We had just returned from an Sunday evening service at Canyon High School. The ministry begun there was not over. The demon was not gone.

We first met this lady at a small seminar held over the weekend in that same cottage. She was a teacher at a local Baptist Christian School. Her newly found interest in the things of the Spirit had drawn her. Blaine Cook, our instructor, was teaching on the subject of healing. After the "lecture" came the "lab", i.e. ministry time. When Blaine invited the Holy Spirit to come all kinds of things began to happen in the packed quarters. Surprisingly our visitor began to shake, swoon and fall to the floor. As Blaine bent down to pray for her he looked up at me and said we had better take her into my office.

Several of us joined with Blaine as he began to minister to her. As he prayed she began to violently resist. Her eyes began to glare at Blaine and in an altered voice told him, "You have no power over me!" Blaine calmly said, "Yes I do." Getting a word of discernment from the Holy Spirit he spoke, "Rage. In the Name of Jesus leave her!" With a shudder it was gone. The same process was repeated with "Bitterness." When "Abuse" manifested Blaine looked at me and said, "Eddie, its your turn." Whoa! I thought to myself. This is for real! Under the Spirit's anointing I followed Blaine's model and it worked. Another unwelcome visitor departed. Once freed the young lady wept tears of great relief and joy. But the story doesn't quite end there.

The next day we took her to Canyon High for the evening service. Unexpectedly she became agitated during worship, requiring us to take her to their ministry room. The prayer team had no success in freeing her from this last dark stronghold. When the lights went out as the service ended we realized that she would be driving home with us, along with an unwanted and unseen passenger. Sort of like being in the old Haunted House ride at Disneyland where a holographic ghost was projected alongside you in your seat.

Feeling desperate, I chased down John Wimber. Finding him in the parking lot, I pleaded with him to impart to me some more anointing for what was soon coming. John graciously laid hands on me and imparted a new authority and power to minister in the kingdom of God. The results of that prayer would be needed in a few minutes but would remain with me for many years to come.

Upon our return on that stormy night Janet and I began the long struggle to set our new found friend free. Taking turns, we prayed for what seemed like hours. Without some of the more sophisticated tools we would learn in the future we had to lean heavily on the powerful Name of Jesus, speaking in tongues and shear endurance. I think this unclean spirit just got tired of our yelling and perhaps our bad breath. It quietly disappeared. When the three of us exited the cottage and walked her to her car we were all basking in the peaceful presence of Jesus and praising him. He had set her free. She was free indeed!

Now all this deliverance business was a bit new to me. I was coming from a naive Christian position that believed all the demons lived only at the time of Jesus or were far away in deepest and darkest Africa. Certainly not to be confronted here in the United States unless you were dealing with the occult. But the Canyon High meetings gave me a new perspective on what happens when the kingdom of light encounters the kingdom of darkness. During one of the first worship sessions ever attended there I looked down from the bleachers to see a man begin to shake and then do a backflip over the chairs. When he landed several rows back he was shaking convulsively and coughing. The ministry team closed in and rushed him into the back room where he experienced a powerful deliverance.

John's teaching on what happened to Jesus when he preached his first sermon in Capernaum shed lots of light on this incident:

"Then he went down to Capernaum, a town in Galilee, and on the Sabbath he taught the people. They were amazed at his teaching, because his words had authority. In the synagogue there was a man possessed by a demon, an impure spirit. He cried out at the top of his voice, "Go away! What do you want with us, Jesus of Nazareth? Have you come to destroy us? I know who you are—the Holy One of God!" "Be quiet!" Jesus said sternly. "Come out of him!" Then the demon threw the man down before them all and came out without injuring him. (Luke 4:31-35)

John shared how when the presence of Jesus comes by the Holy Spirit demons are forced to reveal themselves. We shouldn't be surprised by that. That's what we saw with the Baptist school teacher and in the gymnasium church service. He illuminated the language of the text by explaining that when Jesus said, "Be quiet!" it was a a forceful command as if to choke off the demons activity, telling it to "Stop it!" And then to "Get out!." We would apply this simple sequence in the many situations that were soon to come our way. John often said, "Jesus never met a demon he liked!" We picked up the same attitude.

In the weeks that followed, during one of our services in our fledgling San Clemente Vineyard a woman got up during the worship and went to the restroom saying she felt ill with pain in her abdomen. Talking with her after the service she introduced herself as a professional medium in search of deeper spirituality and physical healing. We were invited to come to her home to pray with her.

In her living room she reported to us that she suffered from painful fibrous cysts. We asked her about her work as a medium. She said she consulted a spirit-guide called Rosa who gave her information about her clients. I asked her if Rosa was present right now and she said that she was actually hovering in the corner of the ceiling. I sensed that was a deception and the demon was actually in her. I explained to her the dangers of being involved with occult practices and the salvation found in Jesus. She was not interested but would still like prayer.

As we began to pray for her healing the demon inside her manifested, contorting her face into a strange, animal-like shape. A deep, masculine voice began speaking to us warning us to back off. When the woman felt her face torque and heard the foreign voice she immediately cried out to Jesus for salvation. She renounced her occult activities. We commanded the unclean spirit to leave. The demon shrieked and left. Several others were cast out in the following days. During one deliverance session her atheistic husband was awestruck and gave his life to Jesus. Soon after all the cysts disappeared and she regained her health.

We soon learned that spiritual warfare is a two-way street. Like in a football game there are times when you are on the offense and then times when you are on the defense. When there is a forceful positive kingdom action there can be a forceful negative reaction from the dark side.

Soon after the Rosa affair a transient prophet showed up at the church office. In an attempt at hospitality I invited him home for dinner. I was a bit disturbed when he began to prophecy over my younger son. Saying first some good things about him and then stranger and more negative ones. After dinner he came with me to our mid-week meeting. In the middle of worship he got up on stage and began to prophecy over the musicians. Then, grabbing the microphone, he spoke strange things over the congregation. Finally, my spiritual antennae picked up from the Holy Spirit discernment that this was demonic. With my elders help we had to escort him out and ask him to leave.

That night as I lay down to sleep a cloud of pervasive darkness came over me, filling my mind with many fears especially concerning my son. I became nauseous and disoriented. I panicked and called John on his home phone. I told him about the strange visitor and asked for prayer. He told me to put my hand on my chest and then he commanded the evil spirit to lift off of me. I literally felt a wave of the Spirit come upon me. I looked down and saw my t-shirt ripple, starting at my abdomen, moving up my chest and then felt a dark presence flow past my face and leave.

Immediately the fear and nausea left. I asked John what was that? He simply said, "You got slimed!" It was a priceless lesson on learning defense as well as offense in the kingdom of God.

As time went on I foolishly began to think I was becoming somewhat of an expert on deliverance. However, John always warned us not to think of ourselves as experts in any field of healing - only general practitioners. I learned that lesson the hard way. While participating as a ministry team member at one of John's healing seminars in New York I was called to another back room. There a dozen people surrounded a man who was standing on a chair angrily roaring at them. People were shouting the Name of Jesus, waving their Bibles and commanding the demon to go. With the situation worsening I stepped in and took over. But my "superior skills" were to no avail.

Just then John stuck his head in the door. Walking in, he motioned everyone to calm down and take their seats. The place went dead silent as John waited on the Holy Spirit's directions. After several minutes he simply asked the man if his father had abused and abandoned him. The man paused, bowed his head, said yes, and burst into tears. John moved in closer and embraced him. The man continued to cry convulsively until he went still in John's arms. I was so embarrassed. John motioned to me and we walked out together. In the hallway he said, "Eddie, not everything that looks like a demon is a demon." A lesson I never forgot.

One year later I was standing before 1,500 people at Westminster Central Hall in London. Along with Becky Cook, I was teaching a workshop on deliverance. In the front row were major leaders in the Anglican Church who were attending John's Signs and Wonders Conference. Many were Oxford dons. When I look back at a picture taken there I can hardly believe I was in that position. However, that's the way it was in "Classic Vineyard," always flying by the seat of your pants. Often tossed into the fray by John. Always being just one page ahead of those you were teaching. When Becky and I invited the Spirit of Jesus to come, He came, demons manifested and we did our best to cast them out.

In the years that followed we experienced the full array of deliverance experiences. John's insight on the technical language of deliverance shed light on them. He taught that the greek word for "demon-possessed" (daimonizomai) could better be translated "demonized." The scope of "demonization" ran the gamut from causing a fever (Luke 4:39) to total inundation as seen in the Gadarene demonic.(Luke 8:27) While we found "possession" rare; "problematic influence" was not. Certainly not all physical, emotional or spiritual sicknesses are directly demonic but sometimes they are. The Spirit usually provides the discernment to tell the difference. Spiritual warfare demands spiritual awareness, ministry with eyes wide open.

Thirty years later I no longer consider myself on the frontline of kingdom signs and wonders expansion and its been a while since dealing with an actual talking demon. But just this summer as I was teaching on contemplative prayer in a leadership conference I discerned a deliverance had taken place. As the group entered a time of contemplative prayer they entreated Jesus to have mercy on them, the Holy Spirit to come in power and Abba, Father to find them in his Love. Then they all waited is silence in the Lord's presence.

In the sharing time afterwards, a woman told us of having experienced serious intestinal pain throughout the previous night. It was still bothering her when we began the meeting. But during the prayer exercise she felt the Spirit's power pass through her body, a pressure build in her abdomen and then burst as a dark presence left her. Instantly the pain was gone. Light and love flooded her being. I guess John's impartation prayer over me in the parking lot is still at work.

7

MORRO BAY

The Volvos filled the parking lot of the Inn at Morro Bay, California. They were, after all, the standard for Calvary Chapel pastors. Mine was cobalt blue purchased shortly after planting a Calvary Chapel in San Clemente, a city down the coast. Although I had met Chuck Smith, the founder of the Calvary movement, I considered John Wimber my primary spiritual mentor. At his invitation, I, along with around a dozen other pastors and wives were gathered for what would become our inaugural conference.

There Kenn Gullickson announced that he was turning over his oversight of several churches known as Vineyard Christian Fellowships within the Calvary movement to John. With that, John told us of Chuck Smith's recommendation that he align himself with Ken and assume the name of Vineyard. In that moment the Vineyard movement as we know it was born. Those of us that wanted to join up could do so simply by changing our name. So we did.

I remember when I returned home and began our Sunday service, I knew I had to make the announcement. Just before I did, I looked out at the face of a man who was a big financial contributor. He often visited our resort town but his home church was Calvary Chapel in Costa Mesa. The Spirit alerted me, "Make that announcement and the money's gone." I did and it was gone. I guess that was my first awareness that there would be a price to pursue the kingdom under the Vineyard banner.

The next year we returned to Morro Bay. That conference contained the three hallmark ingredients of Vineyard tribal gatherings for years to come. There was cutting edge teaching articulating those themes that were on John's mind at the time. There were wide-open "Come Holy Spirit!" times that were very exciting and sometimes made you a little apprehensive. But perhaps the most wonderful thing was the camaraderie that was formed as we all embarked on this wild ride together. When the annual conference was announced each year you signed up with great anticipation.

One of my favorites was called "Wimber on Wagner" where John teamed up with Peter Wagner on the subject of church growth. Peter had written a best-selling book on methods for growing your church. After he taught, John would add his unique spin to it. It was great stuff, but what I remember most were the ministry times. Peter had discovered that he had an unusual healing anointing; that of lengthening legs. So at the beginning of each prayer time he would call people forward who had one leg shorter than the other. He then prayed for each person personally and you know what? Legs grew right before our eyes. We got all excited and had Peter pass on the anointing to us. The theme of that conference was remembered more for growing legs than on growing churches.

It seems like there was always some controversy going on in the Vineyard and the place to address it was the annual conference. In the 1985 conference on prayer John tackled the always interesting topic of bringing down territorial spirits through intercession.

In 1988, we all were enjoying a big BBQ in the parking lot of the Anaheim Vineyard while awaiting a possible decision to sign a document making us an official denomination. Sort of like the people waiting in St Peter's Square for the white smoke from the Vatican when a new Pope is selected. As I recall Carol Wimber had a dream that ended that proposition.

In 1989, we made our way to Denver during the prophetic season of the Vineyard. The conference was gnarly considering the swirling issues. Lot's of powerful personal ministry with revelatory words took place. However, a few words about the death of the Vineyard as we knew it actually caused some to bolt from the movement. In the years that followed John pulled it all back to center.

The conference of 1995 was a thriller as the renewal birthed in Toronto spread though the Vineyard. Certain inexplicable phenomena provided the needed controversy factor. Noted Vineyard scholars like Derek Morphew, Don Williams and Peter Davids were asked to give a balanced perspective. Soon after their positive presentation a person was interviewed about their renewal experience. The person shook in the Spirit and then roared like a lion! There never was a dull moment in those early Vineyard conferences.

In 2002, I retired from the active pastorate and my attendance at conferences waned. But I miss them. And every time someone comes back from one and excitedly says, "It was awesome!" "Radical teaching!" "Boy, did I feel the presence of the Spirit!" "I love my Vineyard tribe!" I smile and say to myself, "Yes!"

8

McCLURE

"Eddie, you're great!" When spoken from the mouth of a man whose smile revealed perfectly white teeth, with that diamond sparkle you see in the movies, I half-believed it must be true. The tone of his voice did seem to resonate in my heart with the spirit of encouragement. He was a modern day Barnabas. His name was John McClure. As a pastor, preacher and prayer-warrior he represented to me classic Vineyard. Everything he did he did wholeheartedly.

I first met John at the Morro Bay conference in 1982 when he, myself and several other Calvary Chapel pastors took on the Vineyard name and John Wimber's leadership. I got to know him much better when later that year a hundred of us went on a mission trip to South Africa. Our goal was to plant a new Vineyard church in Johannesburg. During the days we witnessed in the streets and held outreach conferences in the evenings.

Having been asked to speak at a conference main session, I found myself nervously trying to make myself comfortable onstage. I positioned myself to speak standing behind the electric keyboard, using it as a pulpit, like I had seen John Wimber do at Canyon High School. McClure came up on stage and prompted me to come out from behind the keyboard and stand where everyone could see and hear me better. And of course he said, "You will do great!"

When the conference ended, John, my wife Janet and I decided to take a road trip to Durban on the coast. Crammed together in the backseat of a diesel Mercedes sedan John demonstrated one of his greatest gifts, the ability to sleep at any time, in any place. He closed his eyes and slept almost all of the eight hour trip. Awakening refreshed, he stretched out his arms and of course said, "Isn't it great here in South Africa!"

Coming into Durban we stopped to visit a scenic Zulu village. Thatch-roofed round huts dotted the undulating hillsides covered with sugar cane and thorn trees. After watching native dancers perform, we were invited into the main hut which housed the tribal witchdoctor. Inside we took our places with a dozen others standing in a circle facing the center where stood the feathered shaman. He began to explain his witchdoctor practices pointing out the various pots, vials and bunched plants that he used in practicing his healing arts. He happened to do so perfectly in the Queen's English. It turns out he had a degree from Oxford! He then opened it up for questions. John couldn't resist. His first question was, "Where do you get your power to heal?"

To which the witchdoctor replied, "You're a Christian aren't you? In fact you're a pastor aren't you? I can see an aura of light over you!" John acknowledged that he was a pastor and it was the Spirit of the Lord that rested on him. The shaman went on to explain that a spirit also guided him in all that he did. John then asked if that spirit was here now, in the hut? His answer was "Yes! In fact he lives right over there in that big basket!" I thought to myself, "Whoa, game on!"

"Pastor McClure" was galvanized into action. He proclaimed that the true power to heal was found in the name of Jesus. He explained the Gospel and then closed with an invitation to accept Jesus as Savior. To our surprise the man responded saying that many years ago while at Oxford he had done just that. He even attempted to win his village over to Christ but the backlash of the Devil was so severe that he was forced to give up. What he was doing now was his next best attempt at helping his village. John compassionately offered to pray for him to repent and receive the power of the Holy Spirit, but like the Bible's rich young ruler he declined.

That evening we gathered for dinner at our Durban guest home. Our hosts were related to the man who graciously drove us from JoBurg. They were not believers. Remembering Jesus' instruction to bless a host home with his peace, John asked if we could pray a blessing over the household before we retired to sleep. During the blessing the head of the house received prayer for a chronic illness. In the morning he was elated in waking without his longtime pain.

As we were driving away he came running up to my side of the car. The car slid to a stop on the gravel driveway and I rolled down the window. He asked me if I would pray with him to receive Jesus. I said yes! He prayed. We all left wearing McClure smiles!

That day a gale force wind rocked the ships in Durban harbor. We sought a sheltered beach to take a swim in the warm tropical waters. John and I ventured out and began body-surfing. The strong winds wanted to blow us down the beach toward a submerged reef with vicious waves pounding on it. A warning sign boldly announced this place as "Danger Rocks." Then I noticed John wasn't alongside me. I searched and saw him fifty yards away, adrift towards the rocks. John who had taken off his thick-lensed glasses hadn't a clue where he was. Though in imminent peril he had his usual big smile. I swam over, warned him and we escaped.

On the next leg of that trip a portion of the team went to England for a series of healing meetings. Holy Trinity Brompton, an Anglican church, hosted them. The pastoral staff was Oxford educated, the congregation sophisticated and they were hungry for the Holy Spirit. A perfect environment for John McClure, Vineyard's own "Prince of Preachers." He preached one of the most eloquent, enthusiastic messages on the healing ministry of Jesus that I have ever heard. The room was electric and the response was magnetic. Lines formed to receive ministry.

John wholeheartedly prayed for the sick in his line. His faith was contagious. Many were healed.

As the eighties progressed, the Vineyard grew, and so did its governmental structure. John became a regional coordinator. I served under him as an area coordinator for years. We had many nice lunches at John and Margie's home, making plans, working out problems and praying for one another. John took this stewardship seriously. He invested himself in clarifying Vineyard vision and values. One such example is the Vineyard Statement of Faith, an opus in which he collaborated with Don Williams. John was also intense about beliefs and practices he felt were detrimental.

In 1995, when the Toronto Blessing "roared" through the Vineyard, John was center stage in the controversy it caused. As a Vineyard pastor I attended regional meetings where various issues concerning the renewal were discussed… and debated. John was very concerned about certain "manifestations" and what he called a lack of "intelligibility." As a result he didn't wholeheartedly get on the "Toronto Blessing bus."

As the years passed our paths crossed less but when they did it he was always encouraging. While his focus turned toward his home church and radio ministry, I found myself focusing on conferences, fighting cancer and passing on my church to another pastor. I heard bits and pieces about John facing some challenging circumstances.

Once when preaching at a recent Regional Conference I looked out and there in the front row was John's big smile. Afterwards he greeted me with a classic, "Eddie, You were great!" Later I thought about me being on the stage preaching and John sitting in the seats. It caused me to wonder. What had happened to the man who some thought was the heir-apparent to lead the Vineyard. Had he missed a turn somewhere? What would his legacy be? Divine clarification came soon.

Someone shared with me about the new Archbishop of Canterbury and John's role in his life. In 2013, Justin Selby was installed as the 105th Archbishop of Canterbury, the principle leader of the Church of England and symbolic head of the Anglican Church. In an interview about the circumstances surrounding his decision to go into full-time Christian service he said that it was catalyzed when he attended a Vineyard renewal meeting at Holy Trinity Brompton. And I quote his very words:

"I heard a sermon by John McClure in 1987. He told a story about a time that he had to decide between a fantastic job offer at NASA and the possibility of entering full-time ministry. As he told this story, I sensed God saying, 'That's the choice I want you to make'."[1]

That's so awesome! Now that's the stuff of legacy. I consider myself part of that legacy. John's ministry helped increase the magnitude of my life and many others. That's part of the philosophy of classic Vineyard, each one of us can make a difference, contributing to something bigger than ourselves. Our ministry can increase the magnitude of others.

Last year Janet and I were invited to John's seventieth birthday. We are so glad we went. He beamed when he saw us and our hearts warmed in response. We brought him pictures of us standing together on the windy beach outside of Durban. All smiling.

Just weeks later John suffered what would be fatal injuries from an off-road vehicle crash. He was still going for it...wholeheartedly!

Footnotes:
1. www.alphausa.org, April 11, 2014, Justin Selby interview.

Carolinas restaurant in New York with John and Carol,
Mike Turrigiano and Lonnie.

John and Carol teaching us how to "abound" over dinner.

John applauds the newly baptized in Johannesburg.

John and Margie McClure smiling in New York.

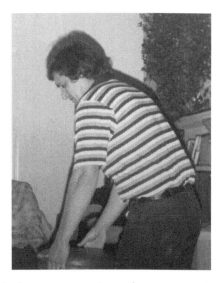

Blaine Cook prepares to introduce us to spiritual gifts.

Janet joins Sam and Gloria Thompson in the Tower of London.

Englishman drunk in the Spirit.

Hanging with Lonnie Frisbee.

Deliverance workshop Westminster Central Hall London.

Team enjoys Oktoberfest in Frankfurt.

Bob Jones prophesies over Mission Viejo Vineyard.

John Barnett before beard with Marie in Montreal.

Dinner with Cooks and John McClure in Vancouver.

Me and Mike Bickle in Kansas City.

Janet getting happy in South Africa tent revival.

Captain John and his first-mate in Oakville, Ontario.

9

CHEERS

After several months of hard work, our mid-week meeting was packing out our rented office space, running about fifty people. The Holy Spirit was moving and kingdom stuff was happening. As a pastor, as things were growing, I was beginning to feel good about myself and this new church plant.

Eager for directions on how to manage this new found success, I called John Wimber who was coaching me at the time. Expecting him to tell me it was time for a bigger building he shocked me with these words, "Break it up!" Inside, I said to myself, "What in the world do you mean, 'Break it up!" He further explained, "Now is the time to multiply small groups." And so, we broke up into four "kinship groups," the name we had for them back then.

Successful small groups are no "slam dunk" as we were soon to find out. In the first year the leaders of two of the groups experienced serious marital issues and as a result their kinships failed. I found myself questioning the "Break'm up" strategy for a while. But the smashing success of the other two overruled my doubts.

Rob and Judy became mother and father to a large group of people from Alcoholics Anonymous. Rob's solid weekly Bible exposition helped objectively stabilize their lives. Judy's tender care gave them a sense of being loved for the precious people they were. One of their men became a well-known lay counselor in the area. Another woman went on to get her masters in psychology and is a professor today.

Jim and Chris, who were very successful business people, gathered all the upwardly mobile, artistic and adventuresome types and shaped them into an on-fire prophetic community. Jim's self-confidence really permitted these creative people to explore their giftedness. Chris's no nonsense presence kept everyone's feet grounded in reality. The two of them became my associates and went on to plant several churches on the East Coast.

During those formative years we benefited immensely from the wise mentoring of senior Vineyard leaders such as Bob Fulton. Bob came and held training seminars for our emerging kinship leaders. His passion for community was downloaded into our spiritual DNA and has never left us. For the next twenty years we would invest in small groups. There were times when we had as many as twenty running simultaneously.

Bob imparted a particular word in his teaching that I have never forgotten: the Latin word, *imago*. He explained that every small group takes on it's unique image. There are no "cookie-cutter" shaped groups. Identifying, cherishing and nurturing that image is of great importance. This insight has been so helpful over the years in mid-wifing the birthing of groups.

John Wimber often reminded us that "people come to a church for many reasons, but they only stay for one: relationship." How often I thought my fine preaching or powerful prayers could do it, but that egoistic desire has sadly been proven wrong. Without making a meaningful relationship within the church people just can't stay. They really need a vital community connection. And only small groups can provide that.

Sam Thompson, one of John's associates, likened the need for small group belonging to the catchy lines from the theme song of Cheer's, the eighties sit-com about friends gathering at a Boston bar. It goes like this:

Sometimes you want to go

Where everybody knows your name,
and they're always glad you came.
You wanna be where you can see,
our troubles are all the same
You wanna be where everybody knows
Your name.

So true. We all need a "Cheers" place in our life. For Mike and Char Turrigiano and members of the Vineyard they pastored, it actually was a bar in Brooklyn, NYC.

Several years after breaking up into small groups, Janet and I, sensing our own need for a Cheer's place, responded to a visiting couple's desire for a Bible Study in their home. There we personally experienced the benefits of being in community.

Our hosts, Frank, a Superior Court judge, and his wife, desired support as they raised their young daughter who was suffering from cerebral palsy. Meeting in their home we all became co-mingled in the ups and downs of their, at times, agonizing situation. Many were the heartfelt prayers of our newfound spiritual family. In the process, Frank, rededicated his life to the Lord. On discovering that he was a runner we spent many miles talking about life while training for marathons. Years later when a family member got in some legal trouble Frank put in a good word for us with the judge. The rewards of relationship.

As with all our meetings we wanted to reflect our core Vineyard values: Worship - Word - Works. Our initial dilemma was we had no worship leader for Frank's group. Once we found out that one of our own played a guitar we drafted him. I remember the first night Dave led worship. He had three songs with chords on three pieces of paper spread out before him. He was doing fine until someone opened the door and a "not-so-mighty" rushing wind came and blew his sheets all over the room. We all had a good giggle, secured the sheets and started over. Dave went on to be a good congregational worship leader. So much multiplication of ministry came out of that little group.

In the years that followed, Janet and I put a lot of energy into starting up new groups, developing new leaders and then letting them take over. One of our greatest success stories was the Sylstra kinship. As I was a life-long surfer I was eager to start a group with a surfing imago, to use Bob Fulton's words. So we pulled together several dozen people from the beach culture. When I was away traveling, Tom Sylstra would step in to lead. Once he threw a backyard party with an Hawaiian roasted pig. It was such a big success that all my disciples declared him the new leader! Tom loved the San Clemente area and would go up on the ridge line overlooking the city and blow the Shofar horn declaring God's coming kingdom.

Tom, a true Renaissance man, surfer, ex-lifeguard, singer, carpenter, clothes-horse, was a very charismatic and caring individual. He, and his wife Melinda, really took care of their little flock. And when it counted, his flock took care of him. Tom was diagnosed with stage four prostate cancer and in the years that followed a beautiful symbiosis of love developed in the group. As members came to pray for Tom he would embrace them and bless them with prophetic words. One of his closest friends, Kevin, kept the cooler full of Corona's to refresh the stream of visitors. When Tom passed we celebrated his life with an "Aloha Tom" memorial and blew the Shofar.

It has been sixteen years since Tom left us but we have not forgotten him. One of his grand-daughters blew the Shofar this year, as she does every year, at our Easter service in San Clemente. Almost everyone in the Sylstra kinship was there.

Small groups often bear big fruit both in the short and the long term. The Hudgins kinship did both. It was birthed when Mike Hudgins, a missionary and disillusioned former pastor visited a small group for new people at our Mission Viejo Vineyard. Mike had reluctantly attended but was surprised when the Holy Spirit fell on him as I prayed for him. The resultant renewal of the Spirit led Mike to join the church and start a small group of his own, eventually becoming an associate pastor in charge of, what else, small groups.

Several years later his kinship, bearing the imago of people passionate for missions, was bursting at the seams. Simultaneously Mike felt called to plant another Vineyard, like ours, across the valley. We blessed him and his people and sent them out. The new church thrived.

Two years after the plant I was diagnosed with leukemia and was in a battle for my life. After another two years I was in remission and on the road to recovery. However, the struggle had taken the wind out my sails. One day Mike and I ran into each other in the aisle of a supermarket. It turned out to be a divine appointment that led to a merging of our two churches.

You never know where "Break it up!" can lead!

10

THE PROPHETIC

It was a strange scene. A dozen of us were sitting in a circle eating barbecue beef sandwiches, trying to keep the sauce from dripping on our clothes. The heavy-set, silver haired man sitting across from us wasn't as concerned. He simply wiped the excess off with the back of his hand. So this was the prophet we had heard so much about? This was Bob Jones?

We were part of a Vineyard team backing up John Wimber at his 1985 Signs and Wonders Conference in Kansas City. Our assignment was to do a follow-up satellite conference at Kansas City Fellowship. The rumor was that there were prophets there. Real Old Testament types, who could "read your mail" and give you a "word from the Lord!" But by his looks Bob Jones didn't fit the profile. That is until he spoke.

He looked across the circle at me and said, "Eddie, the Lord showed you to me ten days ago." And inside I said to myself, "Sure!" But then he began to describe in detail many of the events that had led me to participate in the conference, including personal conversations with the Lord that no one knew about but me. That got my attention! I then asked him, "So, Bob, what did the Lord show you."

He said, that in a vision he was standing with Jesus, looking down from a heavenly vantage point, and saw me standing in a hallway with dozens of people passing by. I was holding a door open and telling everyone, "The Father loves you! Come into His house!" Those that entered went first to the bathroom, to be cleansed, and then went into a beautiful banquet room with a waiting feast. Bob then said to me, "Eddie, you're the Lord's Doorman. Tens of thousands will pass through that door and come to experience the Father's love."

The word resonated with my spirit but made no sense to my mind. For at that time, I had not yet had my watershed experience of the Father's love. That would come months later. So as John had taught us, I put this word "on the shelf," trusting that if it was from the Lord, he would bring it to pass. As it turns out, it was, and some thirty years later, many tens of thousands have passed through that door.

Prophetic activity was certainly not foreign to us in the early days of the Vineyard. John regularly taught that the use of spiritual gifts was part of our supernatural kingdom activity. They were the "tools of the trade" so to speak. Seeing visions and speaking prophetic words were routine in our gatherings. We were encouraged to run the risk of being wrong and learn how to use them effectively. Classic Vineyard provided a learners climate.

My first prophetic word came at a small pastors retreat that John and Carol were hosting in Anaheim. During one of our meetings, I had a vision of a huge hand reaching down out of the sky and picking up an old, rusty sledgehammer buried in the desert sands. Trembling, I blurted out what I saw with these spontaneous words following; "The Lord is reaching down from heaven and lifting up burned-out, discarded pastors, and will powerfully use them to break the chains of those the enemy is holding prisoner." I remember Carol got excited and said, "Eddie, that was a good word!"

So many good words were given in those days. Brent Rue, a Vineyard pastor in Lancaster, California had a lot of them. In 1982, at a pastors meeting in South Africa, he spoke a word over me; "I see a barren field with one lonely sunflower. Now I see a field flowing with golden sunflowers. Eddie, you are that flower and you will be multiplied." An encouraging word to a pastor attempting to plant a new church. Five years later, as I was emerging from a painful downturn that occurred when moving the church to a new location, Brent came up to me with another word. He said, "I see a barren field with one lonely sunflower..." And you can guess the rest. When I asked Brent if he remembered the previous word, he said he had no recollection of it. But

I did. It was a very good word that made a big difference in encouraging me to carry on.

Fast forward to 1989, and the Spiritual Warfare Conference in Anaheim. The roster was filled with all the usual suspects of Vineyard speakers. I was scheduled for a workshop. Showing up just before the opening session, I ran into John in the hallway. He asked me to step into his office for a moment. Turns out it was a big moment. He told me that a prophetic man by the name of Paul Cain had recently visited him. This man told him that his coming would be accompanied by an earthquake occurring at a very specific time. Apparently this happened. The prophetic message he brought to John was that the Vineyard was in need of a course correction, that certain leaders were in sin, and that John needed to discipline "his children" so to speak. And if he did so, his prodigal son Sean, would return home, which did happen later.

John informed me that Paul, Mike Bickle, and others from Kansas City would now be the principle speakers, and that he was in the process of canceling the scheduled Vineyard speakers. However, when he came to my name, the Lord spoke to him telling him not to cancel my workshop. This turned out to be of immense importance to me. It was at that workshop I would present for the first time a systematic teaching on the Father's love. From that one workshop would come speaking invitations that lasted for over twenty years.

The teaching and ministry from the main sessions in that conference ignited a firestorm of controversy. On one hand, there were some powerful anointed messages on repentance and incredible times of personal prophetic ministry that changed lives and launched ministries. On the other hand, a "prophetic paradigm" emphasizing the need for extreme holiness and intercession in order to facilitate the next "big move of God" was problematic for some.

I remember taking a coffee break with Ken Blue and Kevin Springer and listening to them discuss the potential problem of drifting towards what they called the theology of the "Latter Rain Movement" or the "Manifest Sons of God." Although I was not familiar with either, I had sensed some personal dissonance also. Our historic focus on the "now" aspect of the kingdom of God seemed to be forgotten with the emphasis on the "not yet" dimension. Prophetic teaching focused on preparing for the future took up most of the conference space leaving little room to pray for people to be healed or filled with the Holy Spirit right now.

In the years that followed, the Father's love began to emerge as my life message. For a while I traveled with John, Paul and Mike Bickle. They would preach primarily on holiness related subjects and I on the love of the Father. The ministry times were distinctly different. Most were filled with cries of repentance while mine seemed to be with tears of love.

One day John gave me a call at home and told me that although he believed that the Spirit was blessing what I was doing, he himself didn't quite understand the message, and was afraid that it was not harmonious with the main themes of the conferences. With his fatherly blessing, I was released from the conference schedule. Although I was disappointed, I soon realized that it was for my good, and the growth of my heavenly Father's love in my life. Carol recently shared with me that it was John's lack of having a father that hindered his grasp of the Father's love, but that "near the end of his life the Father revealed it all to him and he became a different man…he was beautiful."

Taken off the stage for a time, I was out of the line of fire in the tense years that followed. For several years there were huge worldwide conferences on holiness with powerful moves of the Holy Spirit. While there is no doubt that many benefited from this focus it was a drift from the "main and plain" Vineyard focus of "equipping the saints" for the work of the kingdom. Subtly the onus for prophetic ministry shifted to a highly gifted few. Dissonance increased.

John Wimber operated with the philosophy of letting new perspectives grow, like a new bush, within the Vineyard movement. This kept us participating with what the Spirit was doing in the Church at large. After a period of time of "letting a bush grow", he would reassess it and "trim the bush" as necessary. When philosophical problems arose with certain prophetic activities and agendas, John met with the prophetic leaders, whom he considered to be fine men. He told them that he had decided to rededicate himself, and the Vineyard, to its primary calling of equipping the saints for ministry. The "prophetic bush' was trimmed and trimming is never tidy.

In the meantime, off the main stage and out of the "big river" of controversy, I stayed home in our Mission Viejo Vineyard and began seminars on the Father's Love. I appreciated being in the gentle "eddy" to the side of the fast moving current. At home, and on the road, we continued to "do the stuff" embracing the value of the kingdom coming "now". We also gleaned from our prophetic friends the values of revelatory ministry and intercession for the "not yet." As I ministered in both worlds I found that the love of the Father was the "lowest common denominator" making it possible to weather the existential tension between the two. This love reunited John and I in ministry again when the "prophetic season" had passed.

Prophecy itself is timeless. A good prophetic word is always a beautiful thing. It does exactly what the Scripture promises: strengthens, encourages and comforts people. When, in 1998, John Paul Jackson gave me the word "Eddie, you won't die of cancer", little did I know the comfort it would bring a year later when I was battling leukemia. While recently visiting the Anaheim Vineyard, a prophetic word sounded out during the silence after worship and we all felt the power of the Spirit invigorate us. The other day, while conversing with a fellow surfer in the line-up, he told me how Mike Hudgins, pastor at the Vineyard in Laguna Niguel, had prophesied over him and gave him words of hope, encouraging him in the midst of a devastating personal crisis. Good words, still coming, with good results!

Several years ago I was on an evening walk and ran into an old acquaintance named Scott. He was taking out the trash in front of a new home under construction. As it turns out, Scott was the contractor, and this was a home he was building for speculation. He told me of his concern about how the recent economic slowdown might force him to take a big loss on the project. As he spoke, the verse Jeremiah 29:11 came to mind, "I know the plans I have for you, declares the Lord, plans to prosper you and not to harm you." I shared this scripture as a prophetic word of encouragement. In the years that followed he ended up selling his old home and moving into the new one. A definite upgrade. However, in those challenging times, work was scarce and paying the mortgage was hard.

At one of our recent early morning prayer meetings we spent some time silently waiting for prophetic words from the Lord. I received a mental picture of a Monopoly "get-out-of-jail" card. Sensing this was for Scott, I shared it with him. Turns out that the day before as he was playing with an old Monopoly game, he picked out that same card, and set it on his mantle. A couple days after the prayer meeting he received a lucrative contract that got him "out of jail" and out of debt.

I ran into Scott on my beach walk this morning and told him I had just read Jeremiah 29 in my devotion. His eyes lit up and he said, "Where would I be today if I had not received that word from the Lord? Life is so dog-gone good for us now!"

Whether it is a "big word" from Bob Jones, or my "little word" to Scott, that's the prophetic: getting good words from God and giving them away for good results. Let's all seek God for them, get'm and give'm away!

11

THE FATHER'S LOVE

Many of the early pioneers in the Vineyard were like the "lost boys" in Peter Pan. We were all looking for a lost father's love. Many of us had a dysfunctional relationship with our earthly dads. That was the case with me and my dad. Although my dad was always there and very supportive I never received a hug from him or heard the words, "Eddie, I love you!" He set the bar of performance high for me and when I failed to measure up he expressed his dissatisfaction. Sometimes violently. No wonder I lived with a chronic fear of failure.

I believe John Wimber became a father-figure to me and many others. Beyond his personal Father Christmas looks, he conveyed concern, care and kindness towards us. John never called himself a spiritual father but nevertheless he was. When I reflect on the early meetings at Canyon High School, there was a palpable, warm presence that John identified as God's mercy. In retrospect I might call it the Father's love. John had that anointing of love on his life, and It certainly touched me.

In 1984, I was invited to John's 50th birthday party. Strangely I felt some reluctance in going due to my personal insecurities when around other pastors with larger churches. I could see why they were worthy of an invitation but not me. My wife insisted that I suck it up and get in the car. I'm glad I did. All the notables at the party were so friendly to us. We were even given a place at John's table. On the way home I kept asking Janet, "Why did John invite me? I'm a nobody. Why?" She simply answered, "Perhaps John invited you because he loves you!" Stunned, I echoed, "He loves me?" Then I felt the Holy Spirit come upon me. There was a bursting from some internal well within me and tears began to flow. John's love connected me to the deeper love I was looking for - the Father's love.

On many occasions I heard John teach on Jesus' relationship with his Father at his basic healing seminars. I often used his syllabus at associate conferences and repeatedly taught the material on how Jesus' relationship with his Father was key to his healing ministry. John, chapter 5, where Jesus healed the crippled man at the Pool of Bethesda, was a central text. From there we obtained the famous Vineyard phrase, "We can only do what the Father is doing." But it was verse 20, "For the Father loves the Son and shows him all that He is doing" that captured my attention. If the Father's love was crucial in Jesus' life, how much more in mine?

One late Friday night, following an evening session at a healing conference in Oklahoma City, John and I were in his hotel room, enjoying juicy hamburgers from room service. I was thinking to myself, "It doesn't get any better than this! Ministry and meal with John Wimber, just me and John." Right in the midst of my euphoria John changed the atmosphere. He told me that there was a situation calling him back to the Anaheim church and he would have to leave in the morning. I would need to take his place and finish leading the conference. A knot in my stomach quickly hindered the digestive process. I put my burger down.

Early the next morning, after a fitful night sleep, I went for a jog and upon returning slid into a swirling jacuzzi in an attempt to relax my nerves. Leaning back and looking up into the blue Oklahoma sky I saw jet contrails heading West. Checking my watch, I realized John was on that plane. The knot in my gut returned as I pictured facing the 1,200 people, who would discern immediately that I was not John Wimber! It was at that very moment that I needed to know that John 5:20 was true for me, that the Father loved me and would show me what he was doing.

I lifted my hands to heaven and cried out, "Father, you love me! Father you love me!" I sensed the Holy Spirit fall on me, and felt a warm presence, like liquid love, flow over me and go straight to the knot in my gut, causing it to relax. Then gentle tears followed. I asked, "Oh Lord, what is this?" In my mind I heard, "This is my love for you." That morning, with a new calm and confidence, I stepped up to the conference podium and began to speak.

A few months later, I was at a leadership retreat for our Vineyard church. It was while laying hands on an associate pastor, sending him out to plant a new church that the fear of failure again reared it's ugly head. As I was praying, I had the irrational thought that without this popular assistant the church may not succeed and I would fail as a pastor. This small fear connected to a lifetime of fear and I was suddenly paralyzed by it. But at that dark moment I sensed the presence of light around me and felt a bolt of power hit me. Then I heard, in what seemed like an audible voice, "Eddie, you are my son, I love you. You can never fail in my sight." I fell to the ground as waves of love poured into painful memories draining them of their power. With great relief I began to laugh for a long time. This was my watershed moment in the Father's love.

After several months of working out the theology of my experience, there was an event that launched the revelation of the Father's love into the public arena. During a ministry time at the 1986 Signs and Wonders Conference in Harrowgate, England, a Lutheran pastor went wild in reaction to people praying for him to be filled with the Holy Spirit. He began yelling angrily, pushing people away and knocking over chairs. Attempts to "deliver him" only agitated him more. As I entered the scene I remembered some past lessons learned in tense situations like this and was led by the Spirit to dial everything down. Once everything was calm I made an appointment to meet the man early the next morning.

We were sitting all alone in the front of the empty 2,500 seat auditorium, when I asked him this question: "What are you so mad about?" After pondering the question he answered with gritted teeth, "My father! I hate him!" Spontaneously he told me about experiencing physical and sexual abuse at the hands of his father. He added how he now had problems with sexual immorality and that his marriage and ministry were in shambles as a result. After a while I asked him if he thought he could repent for his sin and forgive his father for his sins against him. He said yes, that's what I want to do.

He prayed a very simple prayer of forgiveness. I blessed his prayer. At that very moment he coughed and a demon left. I then asked the Father to fill him with the love he had never received in life. One tear formed in the corner of his eye. Being a well-trained Vineyard pastor I blessed what the Father was doing. I blessed that tear. It was multiplied. Soon it became a river. Then came the loud cry of a lifetime of pain. It filled the entire auditorium. He wept for a long time until he went silent, completely still and serene. In the evening session, as he worshipped, the Holy Spirit rested upon him and he lifted his arms in peace.

Two years later I was in Berne, Switzerland, for another Wimber conference and was asked to give a little sample of what I would be covering in my workshop on deliverance. I told the story of the Lutheran pastor. As I shared, the Father's love began to move throughout the room touching many. That's when I first sensed there was power in the message of the Father's love. I was scheduled to speak at several main sessions during the following conference in Frankfurt, Germany.

My first session on the subject of deliverance focused on gaining freedom from false father-figures like Adolf Hitler. A gnarly subject to be touching on in the crowd of 7,500. There was a sense of national repentance for the sins of the Fatherland leading to a manifest power encounter where a multitude of captives were set free. But it was at the second session on the topic of inner healing that the Father's love fell, healing and filling thousands of wounded hearts. Loud cries of "Abba Father!" filled the auditorium. The Father was adopting a nation. It was awesome!

This new awareness of the power of the Father's love led to my workshop at the 1989 Spiritual Warfare Conference (which I also talk about in the chapter on the Prophetic.) This was the first time I presented systematic teaching on the subject. As seen in Germany there were powerful deliverances leading to dramatic in-fillings of the Father's love.

One of the many touched there was Carl Tuttle. He was so moved that he invited me to present the workshop material at his church in Santa Maria. It was there I discovered that the message was transferable, not only to the church, but to church leaders. Carl himself began to carry the message into his worship seminars. Thank you Carl for the invitation to come to Santa Maria! It was the first seminar but it led to dozens more over the next twenty years.

When the Spirit fell in the Toronto Vineyard in 1994 the Father's love was embraced as one of the renewal's central themes. Millions have passed through the Toronto doors since then. That renewal touched men like Jack Frost whose teaching on the Father's love touched thousands more. The message has touched so many men, women and ministries, that it now permeates the Church and many missions worldwide.

The year 2016 marks the thirty-first year since I experienced the Father's love and preached the first rudimentary message on the subject in my local Vineyard. In a few weeks I will teach the material one more time at a Vineyard school of ministry. I'm sure I will be surprised again how many people don't yet know how much their heavenly Father loves them but I am no longer surprised at how quickly he comes and pours out his love upon them. He wants them to know they are invited to his party, not because they have done great things, but just because he is a Father who loves them.

12

POWER EVANGELISM

The room was filled with a cacophony of sounds like being in the Enchanted Tiki Room in Disneyland. Only it was not the sound of exotic birds but that of Holy Spirit inspired prayers. Loud cries in the tongues of men and of angels. The prayers of eighty Vineyardites crowded in a hotel room in Johannesburg, South Africa. We were crying out to heaven for a breakthrough here on earth.

Our leader, John Wimber, had just informed us that all the plans for evangelistic ministry in the local schools and university had fallen through. We were here to evangelize, hold interest meetings, and handout invitations to a signs and wonders conference. Now there was no place for us to go during the day for the next three weeks. With all of the investment made for this large team to travel, be housed, and fed, it was a tense moment. John, sensing that there was spiritual warfare at work here, led us into a time of intense intercession. He instructed us to pray as loud as we could in any form we wished, English, tongues, prophecy, spiritual songs or loud shouts. The musicians joined in the rising crescendo until you felt the oppression break and peace flooded the room. John then released us follow the Spirit's leading and go out into the streets.

Janet and I decided to go to the zoo. Even if there were no conversions we could see the cheetahs. So we wandered through the lush oasis of the wild kingdom handing out invitations to the conference. Turning up one gravel pathway we saw a couple sitting on a bench. We felt drawn to go to them and introduce ourselves. Once they knew we were Christians the man asked if we could help them with something. He shared that he and his wife were presently in a severe crisis, financially and relationally. In desperation they had cried out to God for help the night before. That morning they sensed they should read the Bible for the first time. They randomly opened up to the sixteenth chapter of book the book of Acts and read the story of Paul and the Philippian jailor. These verses captured their attention:

He then brought them out and asked, "Sirs, what must I do to be saved?" They replied, "Believe in the Lord Jesus, and you will be saved—you and your household."

Not fully understanding what this meant, they decided to go to the zoo for a walk and try to figure it out. Assuming that we might know, they looked up at us and asked, "Sirs, what must we do to be saved?" After an explanation of the gospel we led them in a prayer to receive Jesus as their

Savior. Immediately the Holy Spirit fell on them. We all left the park hugging and rejoicing. Power evangelism! Yes!

John Wimber defines it like this, "By power evangelism, I mean a presentation of the gospel that is rational, but that also transcends the rational…The explanation of the gospel - the clear proclamation of the finished work of Christ on the cross - comes with a demonstration of God's power through signs and wonders…Power evangelism is preceded and undergirded by demonstrations of God's presence…"[1]

The ministry of Jesus was a model of power evangelism where signs and wonders accompanied his preaching of the gospel. Salvation often was a direct result of a miracle. (The paralytic in Matthew 9 and the blind man in John 9) Power evangelism continued with his disciples in the Book of Acts. (The crippled man healed in Acts 3)

This particular type of evangelism was birthed in the Vineyard following the outpouring of the Spirit on Mother's Day in 1980. Hundreds were converted as a result of empowered believers taking signs and wonders out into the streets. New churches were birthed and a worldwide renewal ministry was launched.

What we experienced in South Africa we took home with us to San Clemente. We held renewal meetings in an "Upper Room" overlooking the city pool. We invited Lonnie Frisbee to come and preach the gospel. One evening a man named Jack came to check things out. He stood at what he thought to be at a safe distance. As Lonnie ministered, the Spirit powerfully fell on Jack. He bent over backward almost touching the ground. He asked those who quickly gathered around him what was happening to him. We answered, "Jack, you are being saved!" He responded by giving his life to Jesus. As it turns out Jack was a significant leader in the local Alcoholic Anonymous. The next Sunday at our fledgling Vineyard he brought three others to church and sat them in the front row.

I will always remember them as the Three Amigos. They were led by Buzz, an Hispanic man with a Pancho Villa mustache. After the message they all came forward during the altar call and were saved. That very day they went to a seminar after church on inner healing where they were filled with the Spirit. One man, Lester, experienced a deep deliverance from alcohol and sexual addiction. Many years later he succumbed to the powers of darkness and suicide but I'll never forget his beautiful salvation and many years of freedom. From that Sunday on there was a steady stream coming from the AA group. Several converts went on to professional Christian positions. Jack and Buzz both continue to this day, some thirty-five years later, to save and shepherd the lost lambs.

While power evangelism is wonderful to see in conferences and the church, it is at its best when seen in your own neighborhood, where you live, work and play.

Tom was my next door neighbor in Mission Viejo. He was the express image of Crocodile Dundee, lean, wiry, weathered, crusty and hawk-eyed. He was the de facto mayor of the street where we lived. He knew the goings-on in everyones lives, including their dirty laundry. He, like Nathaniel, was a man of no guile. He called'm as he saw 'm. But at the core he was very compassionate. He was also a recovering alcoholic.

One afternoon we were hosting a BBQ with friends and having a really good time. Right in the middle of the festivities I heard a voice from the other side of our neighbors block wall, "Eddie, are you there?" As he repeated himself I recognized it as Tom's. Peering over, I saw him leaning against the wall. I could see that he was really quite drunk. He then asked me to come over. I went.

In his kitchen he told me with slurred speech that he had "fallen off the wagon." His wife, fed up with his alcoholism, had just packed up and left. He was in a total panic and near suicidal. He pleaded with me to help him. I told him that he needed more help than I could give him. He needed God's help. His response was that he wasn't deserving of God's help. I explained to him that none of us are deserving, including me and that it is God's mercy that saves us. He still resisted asking God for help.

I asked him if I could pray for him and he agreed. He bowed his head and closed his eyes. I put my hand on his chest and prayed, "Lord Jesus have mercy on Tom." Just as soon as I finished those words the power of God hit him in the chest like a bullet. His eyes sprung open in total shock. He was completely sober and knew it. He reached out his hand to mine and said, "What was that!" "Jesus!" I said. "Jesus is touching you. He is delivering you from the power of alcoholism. He's here right now to become your Lord and Savior. Do you want to pray and invite him into your heart?" He said, "Yes!"

While classic power evangelism usually occurs in these dramatic "point in time" conversions, it can also be seen in the divine providence of events moving people toward conversion. The Bible gives the example of Philip being supernaturally led to encounter the Ethiopian eunuch who so happens to have been led by the power of providence in his reading of the book of Isaiah. When they come together there is an empowered moment of salvation. Being aware that the Spirit is powerfully arranging such "divine appointments" opens the door for many more evangelistic opportunities.

Several years ago I was renovating my backyard and I needed a fence built. I mentioned this to a recently retired friend named Lane who said that he would like a shot at it. He also knew a very skilled woodworker named Branko who would give him a hand. We agreed on a price and the two of them went to work. Branko was a true creative genius when it came to wood but he had a short fuse if someone suggested a modification in his design or methods. Fortunately Lane was a master at soothing his often ruffled feathers. The result of their teamwork was an incredibly elegant redwood fence with a curved gate that would have made Frank Lloyd Wright jealous.

Lane and Branko formed a partnership from that point on. They often worked in close physical proximity. As a result Lane noticed when Branko frequently complained of abdominal pain. When Lane questioned him about it he always changed the subject. One day the pain was so severe that Lane insisted on getting him to the doctors. There he was diagnosed with stage 4 colon cancer.

For the next three months Lane devoted himself to Branko's care, taking him to his chemotherapy treatments, preparing his meals, cleaning his home, etc. Lane set aside his regular surfing activities to serve his friend daily. I have rarely seen such self-sacrifice.

During that time I would occasionally join Lane in praying for Branko. We talked with him about our relationship with Jesus, about the Gospel and God's love for him. He thought Jesus was really good for us but he himself wasn't a believer. But as his conditioned worsened he began to realize that our prayers were bringing him a supernatural peace and comfort in his pain. I think he also began to see the face of Jesus in Lane's compassionate care for him.

Then one morning as we were talking he said that he now wanted what he saw in us. He wanted whatever we had. We told him that he could have it too by simply asking Jesus into his life. Suddenly you could see in his eyes a change of heart. He was wide open to the Lord. He asked us to lead him in prayer. He repeated after us a simple prayer asking Jesus to have mercy on him, forgive his sins, and come into his heart as Lord. And like a little child he was born again. Tears flowed as God's love filled his heart. The fear of death was gone from that moment on. It was soon after that he left us to meet Jesus face to face. My garden gate stands proudly as a memorial of Branko's magnificent entrance into heaven.

The greatest power in evangelism is love. It is the love of God manifest in Scripture, in signs and wonders, in sovereign appointments and in servant-hearts that has the power to convert a person. May the power of that love poured out on the Vineyard on a Mother's Day many years ago continue to flow through us until that day comes when the heavenly mansions are full.

Footnotes
1. John Wimber, Power Evangelism (Chosen, 2014), p. 77.

13

INNER HEALING

My road to inner healing began with a panic attack. After two days of travel, twenty-six hours of flight-time and a ten hour time difference I was trying to go to sleep in my tiny hotel room. My thoughts turned to the realization that I was in South Africa and a really long way from home. I then felt a tinge of anxiety. Hey, if I wanted to go home I couldn't. A wave of fear passed though me. Perhaps it was the little African animal carving I had bought. I got up and put it outside my door. No, that wasn't it. The fear was mounting.

I found temporary relief in a new exit strategy. I would book a flight home in the morning. Whew! But then I thought what a failure it would be on my first mission trip with so much invested. What would my peers think? Wimp? I realized that I couldn't return. I was stuck. At that moment a wave of dark emotion erupted from the depths of my being. Palpable fear. Paralyzing panic. With my head swirling I went out and started pacing the hotel hallways, praying for deliverance. The answer came through a prompting in my mind. Go to the team leader and get him to pray for you. So even though it was quite late I knocked on the door of Sam Thompson.

Fortunately Sam was up, discussing plans for the next day with another team member, Dale Temple. As they prayed for me, Dale got a word of knowledge. He told Sam he believed that this fear had something to do with my relationship with my father. A fear of failure. I would never have guessed that I had a problem with fear. At the time I had never heard of inner healing. But when they began to pray for me I broke out in tears. As I wept I began to feel some relief from the grip of panic. The acute fear began to melt away. I found some peace, returned to my room exhausted and soon fell asleep.

Sam, a psychologist and his wife Gloria, were associates of John Wimber at the church that would become the Anaheim Vineyard. They had oversight of the counseling programs of the church which included the area known as inner healing. On ministry trips they did pastoral training seminars in this area, paralleling the signs and wonders meetings. Being personally focused on the "power" side of the ministry, I didn't fully appreciate the value of their ministry in the beginning. That would change as I gained an understanding of the role of inner healing in kingdom ministry and even more when I saw my own need for it.

The New Testament teaches that our humanity is a unified whole (1 Thessalonians 5:23-24). The in-breaking of the kingdom meant restoration of the body, soul and spirit of man. As a result inner healing had a significant place in Vineyard healing ministry. I just finished re-reading Power Healing by John Wimber and Kevin Springer. There John writes:

"Emotional and psychological hurts linger in the form of bad memories (thoughts of hurtful experiences from the past) and form barriers to personal growth…the healing of these past hurts restores the inward (unseen and unseeable) part of men and women, as opposed to purely physical, visible or outward healing. Therefore the healing of past hurts is commonly called 'inner healing.'"[1]

Of course, like many pioneering focuses in the early Vineyard, inner healing was not without some controversy. Some criticized that it caused people to be too emotional but we were discovering that negative emotions needed processing. Just memorizing Bible verses was not enough. Others felt that it was too commingled with psychology. However, although the Bible is not a psychological textbook, it offers brilliant counsel for matters of the mind, will and emotions. On the other hand there are some valuable truths that God has graciously disclosed in the field of psychology to help mankind. Others said that we need not focus on anything negative from our past lives because we are born again and everything is now made new. For most of us we discovered that not to be entirely true. After many years of working at it, stuff from the past still plagued us.

Inner healing was often an important component of integrated healing ministry. There was an incredible example of this that occurred during a 1985 healing conference in Brighton, England. Responding to a word of knowledge John Wimber had about skeletal deformities, a woman came forward for prayer from the ministry team. Her body was visibly crooked with one shoulder dipped below the other as a result of one leg being several inches shorter than the other. She told us that the bones in her lower back and pelvic area had been malformed from birth.

After praying for some time with no noticeable result, I asked the Lord for direction. Immediately the word "rejection" formed in my mind. When I prayed for the Lord to heal her of any rejection experienced in her life, she screamed out and then slumped to the floor.

Kneeling beside her, I asked if she remembered when she had experienced rejection. She told us a story I'll never forget. "When I was born I had a twin sister who was stillborn at the same time. I had skeletal deformities but was otherwise healthy. These problems put a tremendous financial and emotional burden on my parents. When I was five years old, I was standing outside the kitchen and heard my father say to my mother, ' I'll never understand it. Why did the one with the perfectly formed body die and the one with the deformities live?' I know my father was speaking out of his frustrations with the challenges of caring for me, but nevertheless, it really hurt. I've never been able to forget it."

I explained the importance of forgiving her father as a step in her healing process. I told her that she had a Father in heaven who wanted to touch her with his love and heal the wound of rejection. So she prayed and forgave her earthly father. When we invited the Father to come and minister to her an amazing thing happened!

Tears streamed down her face as the Father's love began to carry away the deep pain of rejection. But as she was crying, I noticed that there was also movement in her body. I reached out and held her heel, praying that the shortened leg would be healed. And then it moved! As her cries of emotional relief deepened, her leg straightened out to its correct length. We asked the Father to pour his love into her whole childhood history. Her bones responded with cracking sounds as the Creator of the world reshaped them. When done, she stood, face tear-stained and shoulders perfectly level.

While I saw more and more people receive deep inner healing little did I know that my own was on its way. Although I had experienced a powerful in-breaking of the Father's love there were still some core issues that needed to be resolved. It usually takes a catalyzing event to put us in touch with these issues. Mine was when my wife served notice that I wasn't the perfect husband I thought I was. At times she felt I was not there for her. I felt rejected. I became reactive. It was a good thing that Sam and Gloria were there for us.

They became the objective third party to help bring objectivity to our swirling subjectivity. With their help we began to get in touch with our emotions and where they were coming from. We both had core issues developed in our childhoods. I had experienced rejection from my performance oriented dad. Janet had deep feelings of abandonment caused by her alcoholic father. These painful issues influenced how we related to each other.

With the Thompson's help we cried out a lot of historical pain and learned how to forgive one another. With new information we changed the ways we related to one another. Through their prayers the presence of the Father's love penetrated deep into our hearts. Inner healing brought wholeness to our lives. And what we learned became our curriculum in counseling a whole lot of others.

Last year we bought two new upholstered chairs for our living room. They replaced a twenty-two year old couch that once sat in my church office. It was a very nice sofa with a beautiful English pattern of green, gold and purple fabric. Over the years hundreds of people, many of them in marriage crisis, sat on that couch and shared their stories with me. Most filled with much pain, misunderstanding and despair. I would listen as Sam and Gloria listened to us. I would offer the wisdom offered us. I prayed as I was prayed for. So many tears shed and absorbed into that fabric.

There is a group of women who meet in our house each week to pray. They are an artistic bunch with an eye for interior decorating. So on one hand they weren't sad to see the old threadbare couch go. But on the other hand it was filled with memories they had of shedding their own tears on it. So they saved one cushion before it departed. They cut the fabric into small squares and had them sandwiched between glass sheets and framed with a golden metal trim. Each woman kept one. They gave one wrapped in ribbon to me. I cherish it. It is like an icon to me. It speaks of the inner healing of the heart. A beautiful thing.

Footnote:
1. John Wimber, Power Healing (Harper One, 1987), p. 80.

14

THE BIG TACO

"But when you give a banquet, invite the poor, the crippled, the lame and the blind." These words of Jesus from Luke 14:13 were the central focus of Fr. Rick Thomas' message to the Vineyard at our 1984 Pastors Conference.

Fr. Thomas incarnated these words through his ministry to the poor who scavenged for food in the dumps outside of Juarez, Mexico. He shared a moving story of how food planned to be enough for 160 people was miraculously multiplied to 300 when providing Christmas dinner. But inspiring beyond the spectacular miracle was the sacrificial, simple lifestyle of Fr. Rick living amongst and serving the poorest of the poor. In fact, even now after his passing, his life is being considered for canonization by the Catholic Church.

Needless to say his presence in the conference helped catalyze ministry to the poor in the Vineyard. It also caused some to consider a simplification of lifestyle. Here's a somewhat related story that I attach to the influence of this conference.

My wife and I went to the conference enjoying our relatively new Volvo station wagon. My wife loved this car. As I drove home from that conference my religious mind began to consider a more modest means of transportation. That Fall when we went to a participate at John's conference in England, I became enamored with the little cars everyone buzzed around in. Albeit from necessity.

Upon our return, I promptly and unfortunately without really weighing my wife's input, dashed off and traded our Volvo in for the smallest Honda Civic. The next year we made our way up the coast to Carmel for a regional pastors conference. As I proudly parked our new austere ride in the hotel parking, I looked back up the entry road. Descending were two brand new Volvo Turbo sedans. One driven by John and the other by his associate Sam Thompson. Somehow I missed the memo. But not my wife's sweet glare. (PS Twenty years later she got her new white Volvo wagon back!)

Fortunately at the time, my associate pastor Jim McDonough had got the right memo. He already had launched an impressive ministry to the poor. When Jim first showed up at our fledgling church plant he wore a three piece suit, had been a success on Wall Street and was on staff for Campus Crusade as a major fund-raiser. But after a couple Sundays he caught the spirit of the Vineyard, started wearing bermuda shorts and began going after the down-and-outers. He, along with his stylish wife Chris, compiled food and clothing donations from local stores and appropriated government food grants. The poor began to show up. And not just outside waiting in lines but sitting in the services…worshipping.

We threw a Thanksgiving Dinner for our congregation with a primary focus on inviting all the needy who had been receiving help. Of course there was not enough food and the Lord rose to the occasion and multiplied it! What a diverse group the needy were. Jim lovingly called them the "Star Wars Space Bar." One mentally challenged lady, who wandered the streets for years, always managed to show up in the latest fashion. Another, called "Tall Richard," was a gangly 6'6" with a huge smile which betrayed missing teeth. His traveling companion, "Short Richard," was 5'5" and his eyes wandered in different directions when he looked at you. But all three loved Jesus, loved to contribute their insights on life and loved to serve in the food ministry.

When we moved the church to Mission Viejo, Jim left to plant a new Vineyard in New York and the Lord sent Rod Stinson to carry on this benevolence work. Rod had graduated from Fuller Seminary and was anxious to be mentored in Vineyard ways and then be sent to plant a church in Russia. His plans were changed for a season when he had a startling vision. He saw a "big taco" suspended in the sky. It didn't take him long to interpret this as a call to start a food ministry to Hispanic people.

Rod began by bringing lunches to the day-laborers standing around waiting to be hired. Then he branched out to feeding their families. We again contacted local markets and government agencies for resource. Soon we had to rent a a warehouse to receive pallets of surplus food that had to be sorted out. Our church families would gather on Saturdays to cull out rotten fruit, leaking cans and jars with strange molds inside. Real hands on stuff.

The "big taco" revelation paid additional dividends when we planted an actual Hispanic church. Andy Brown and his wife Cathy were missionaries in Guadalajara Mexico who had returned to the U.S. They joined the church and picked up the baton from Rod. They took food out to needy families and then held local block parties with music and preaching. From there they planted our La Vina congregation which is thriving over twenty years later.

When we moved the church into a converted movie theatre we dedicated the basement to benevolence ministry. Soon some local transients joined in the food lines. There were two interesting fellows who were living in the canyon next to our property. They had a cardboard enclosure, a campfire to cook food and regularly bathed in the creek. On one fine Summer afternoon I saw them soaking in two stream-side holes they had dug as makeshift jacuzzis. With faces lifted to the sun, getting a nice tan, they munched on cheese and crackers from the warehouse.

On Sundays they spruced themselves up and hiked up the bank to the church. They were first in line for coffee and doughnuts. Both had Bibles and a good working knowledge of the Word. They were a welcome part of the congregation until one afternoon the county trucks showed up and whisked them away. Walden Pond was no more.

When I retired from the senior pastorate our benevolence ministry morphed into a 50,000 square foot facility called Mercy Warehouse, under the visionary leadership of Mike Hudgins, pastor of Vineyard Community Church in Laguna Niguel, Ca. It feeds and clothes thousands of the local poor. From it, huge containers are filled and shipped to South Eastern Asian nations in need.

Both Mike and I were greatly influenced by a man named Victor Klein who had an incredible heart for the poor. He had a dream of building a supply center sending ships of food and medical supplies to Asia. He invested hundred of thousands of dollars to that end. Mercy Warehouse is the fulfillment of his vision.

Now back in my hometown San Clemente, I've experimented with some small church services in a local pub called Molly Bloom's. In one of our last meetings a transient man wandered in. He had heard Jesus attended the meetings. He silently stole into a back seat but was immediately escorted to the front. Sitting next to me, he introduced himself as Eddie. Small world. He sat with eyes closed during the worship. Soon he was trembling and teary eyed. He took communion and listened intently to my little homily. Afterwards several of us stayed and had lunch. Eddie ate his fill and smiled.

PS: John didn't keep the Turbo Volvo very long. Through the length of his pastorate at Anaheim, he and Carol brought food to their warehouse ministry and helped pass it out to the poor. I was impressed with how they brought their grandkids along to help. Just several weeks ago Carol had to break away from an after-church conversation because it was her turn to help distribute to the needy.

15

RENEWAL

In January of 1994 I was hearing rumors of renewal breaking out in a Vineyard church in Toronto, Canada. It just so happened that I was scheduled to lead a Father Loves You Conference in that area in April. As renewal was in the DNA of classic Vineyard, I decided to pay a visit the night before our conference began.

The Toronto Airport Vineyard was housed in a nondescript, industrial-type building near the airport. Inside there were a couple hundred people seated in front of a typical looking worship band. Worship was good. The presence of God was palpable, but nothing out of the ordinary happened. Then the pastor, John Arnott, gave a basic and brief Bible message. At it's conclusion he invited a young man forward to give a testimony.

Though young, his weathered face and a somewhat emaciated body betrayed a hard life. He gave an eloquent testimony of coming to know Jesus as his Savior during a recent renewal meeting. John asked if he could bless him and he responded in the affirmative. As John laid hands on him the Holy Spirit came upon him, mildly at first and then what looked almost violently. The man began to bounce up and down on the seat of his pants. He cried at first but soon a smile came on his tear-stained faced and he broke out in laughter. I was wide-eyed, wondering what in the world was going on.

John began to interview him about what he was experiencing. The young man began to cry again and tell us of his terrible childhood relationship with his father and then his tormented life of addiction. He said that when the Spirit came on him he felt power breaking chains to free him from his bondage. Then it all changed when he felt the warmth of love envelop him and a voice tell him that he was loved. John then asked him the question that was on all our minds, "What was going on when you were bouncing all over the floor?" His answer? "I saw my Heavenly Father bouncing me on his lap!"

As I sat there, my analytic mind was doing its work in evaluating what I had just seen, trying to discern the validity of the renewal taking place here. As in any other meeting I was looking for three things: the saving message and ministry of Jesus, the manifest power of the Holy Spirit, and, especially for me, the demonstrated love of the Father. All three were here "in spades."

At the close of the meeting John invited forward anyone who wanted to receive from the Spirit's outpouring. Janet and I, along with some of our staff members, always hungry for more, stepped up for prayer. John and Carol Arnott laid hands on us and soon we were laid out on the floor. That is, all except my wife, who has always been a bit more circumspect than me. It took her some time to soak it all in before she, in a lady-like way, took the supine position.

While on the floor I had a vision of myself holding assorted gift-wrapped packages in my arms. Then a Fatherly voice whispered in my ear, "I have given you unique gifts and it is all right to use them." These words were very timely to me because I had recently declared to my church that we would pursue being a "presence-driven" church. We would allow all the gifts of the Spirit to be used in our meetings. This was a risky position for a church meeting in a "purpose-driven" section of Orange County. This loving affirmation from the Father, indicating he knew how I was spiritually gifted, touched me deeply.

The next Sunday, back at my home church, I shared about our Toronto experience. At the end of the service I told the congregation that I wasn't sure if what we received was transferrable but I would like to pray and see. Everyone stood to receive. I raised my hands and blessed them to receive whatever had been imparted to us. I went down from the stage and laid hands on the first row. The Spirit fell on many just like it did to us in Toronto. As I progressed down the middle aisle moving toward the rear, row after row were powerfully touched. I actually felt like a "western gunfighter" projecting powerful "bullets of the Spirit." When I got to the rear of the church I turned around to see what looked like a war zone with hardly a body standing. My first thoughts were, "Oh My God, What have I done!"

That Sunday began several years of renewal in our church. For the most part they were wonderful years. From my point of view I saw the primary thing that was happening was a massive outpouring of the Father's love. Regardless of the physical manifestations I always tried to look past them and see what was going on inside the person for a manifestation of the Father's love. I must admit that it took a lot of work to sort out the wheat from the chaff, but in the end it was worth it.

Many of the more explainable manifestations were not foreign to me. They often accompanied renewal meetings I participated in with John Wimber. In those meetings we saw the Holy Spirit "fall" in power. Many people were overwhelmed and fell to the ground. Cries and tears of healing were commonplace. Even shrieks and shaking bodies of those being delivered form bondage. I saw a man in England, who had not slept flat on a bed for many years because of scoliosis, turn into "The Rubberman " before my eyes, and then jump up and run around the room laughing for half an hour.

Even laughing was not unusual to us. Once, at the final session of a conference, John prayed for an impartation of the Spirit's anointing. The immediate result was a silent pause, then a pocket of laughter broke out. It eventually spread to the entire audience. John commented that sometimes all we need is a good laugh.

Now I know that some manifestations, especially animal sounds, were a bit disconcerting, and really beyond any dualistic definition. I found that they actually faded after the initial outpouring. I have returned to Toronto many times over the years and no longer see them, but back then they brought controversy and criticism from certain elements of the Church. We took a lot of local and not so local flak for hosting the renewal.

In the quest of explanation I invited Todd Hunter, who at the time was a major leader in the Vineyard, to speak at our Sunday night service. The place was packed with hundreds of people. Todd gave an eloquent discourse on historical renewal. When finished he invited people forward to receive prayer. They responded by rushing the front and packing the space below the stage. Todd prayed, the Spirit fell, and most everything that could happen …happened. I thought it was awesome!

However, one problem occurred when Todd bent over to pray for the people. His lapel microphone remained on, and everything was recorded. When the tapes of his message went out, the sounds of the ministry time went with them. The sounds most dominant were of those people at the front, who were the most enthusiastic and responded with the greatest drama. To listen to that short part of the tape, without being aware of the larger context could be alarming. Unfortunately, a local renewal critic got hold of the tape and played it on Christian radio across the entire country. He introduced it by saying that it was recorded at the Mission Viejo Vineyard and that the sounds heard on the tape could only be heard elsewhere in an insane asylum.

The renewal became the central focus of the Vineyard International Conference at Anaheim in 1995. John interviewed some Vineyard theologians on their viewpoint and to the surprise of many they were positive about it with some minor qualifiers. The ruffled feathers of many with concerns were calmed down. However, they didn't stay calm for long. A woman, who happened to be from our church, was brought up on stage and was interviewed about her renewal experience. When she received prayer she "roared like a lion" in front of couple thousand people. Feathers started ruffling again.

What some explained as "prophetic manifestations" continued to polarize viewpoints on what was being then called The Toronto Blessing. Another issue of concern was the lack of evangelism, healing ministry and church growth that some failed to see in the renewal. John Wimber, who I believe was weary from the recent prophetic controversy, as well as battling health issues, found it necessary to clarify the Vineyard position. He called for a return to the "main and plain" of Vineyard values: that of equipping the saints for the work of the church and church planting. Renewal would not be the central focus. John Arnott felt called to continue the renewal focus. A separation ensued.

We continued to embrace the renewal in the years that followed while simultaneously pursuing doing the works of the kingdom. We found balance by centering on the experience of the Father's love, which empowered us within and further equipped us to move out into the community and the world. There were several of our staff members who spent many hours "soaking in the Spirit" who later were sent out to plant churches. Many gifted people enhanced by the Spirit stepped into full-time ministry positions.

Due to my life message of the Father's love I have been invited to speak at many events sponsored by Toronto Airport Church, which is now known as Catch the Fire Toronto. Their movement has adopted the Father's love as a major theme. Whenever I teach I am asked to include a presentation of the Gospel and a time for people to respond. Usually before I speak there is a time of praying for the sick. It's cool to see them doing the stuff we ourselves value so highly. John and Carol Arnott have become good friends. However, I am always introduced as: "Ed Piorek - a Vineyard pastor."

16

MINISTRY TEAM

It was very dark, and cold, when we emerged from the train station around midnight. Our English guide hurried us up the steps leading to the parking lot. As we were exiting, I turned and read the big black letters illuminated on the white sign overhead: Potters Bar. Crowding into a couple tiny sedans, the eight of us freezing Californians rumbled off toward town and our waiting host homes.

Our car pulled up in front of a typical English row house. Two stories, brick facade and aluminum framed windows. The windows were dark. There was no welcoming light left on for us. We were told the door would be unlocked. So, Janet and I stepped inside the empty house, to find a note sitting on a table. It instructed us that we would find our room ready at the top of the stairs. Our hosts had gone to bed.

Opening the door and turning on the light, we gasped a little, looking at the two small and very thin futons on the floor. A blanket and a pillow lie on each one and the wall heater was turned off. It was icy. Janet and I made like eskimos and cuddled together under the covers until dawn.

In the morning, we met our hosts, two quintessential English spinsters. Both a little portly, with wiry hair and dressed in what I would call, weathered wool skirts and sweaters. Their eyes seemed to dart around under their glasses. They were a bit strange, and I'm embarrassed to confess, that I nick-named them Tweedle Dee and Tweedle Dum. They were members of the local Anglican church, although they rarely attended. So, when we left for Sunday services they stayed at home.

The little church was a Gothic beauty with its stone and stained glass. The service was traditional Anglican. The vicar in robes, the incense, bells, wafer and wine. There were a few dozen in attendance, most over sixty, which seemed quite old to us then. During the announcements, the vicar introduced us as the Vineyard team here to do followup ministry after the John Wimber Signs and Wonders Conference in London. At the conclusion of the formal service, the congregation was invited forward to receive healing prayer.

So, there we stood, Janet and myself, Marti, Eddie, Denise, Neal, Glenn and Sheila. The eight of us were the "ministry team." Fortunately only eight people came forward. The woman Marti was praying for got upset because she was chewing gum as she prayed. I asked the lady,

"Well, did you get healed?" Her answer? "Yes!" A person healed! That's the reward of being on the ministry team, the reward for a freezing room without a view in Potters Bar.

Our little team had already been well rewarded the prior week at the main conference in London. We were part of a big team from the Unites States praying for the hundreds coming forward for healing. We ministered to many people there with some amazing results. One in particular stands out. I'll let Marti tell it in her own words:

"From the stage, John Wimber gave a word that was very specific. He said, "If the Lord has spoken to you this week and told you that He's going to heal you, come forward now." The ministry team was then given instructions to pair up by twos and fill the aisles and wait for the people to come. I loved this word! This was going to be so easy! The Lord has already promised to heal these people. This was going to be great!

And then, we saw them. They were a group of three slowly making their way up the aisle towards us. An older woman to his right, and a young man to his left leading a very obviously blind man up to the spot where we stood. The young man explained that the blind man was his father who had lost his sight due to diabetes. He introduced the woman on the other side as his mother. He further explained that the Lord had spoken to him that he was going to heal his father at this conference.

At this point, I was a little detached from the proceedings, trying to listen for a word or a whisper from the Holy Spirit. What I did not know was that Eddie had already heard from God. "They have the faith of the bed carriers." So we began our prayers, again with Eddie leading. I was glad he was doing the heavy lifting as I was asking the Lord for faith to even be involved in this. "Lord give me faith," I prayed silently.

At that moment, John had a word from the stage, "Right now, the Lord is healing a man blind from diabetes." I turned to look at John. The crowd roared as a wave of faith filled the room. When I turned back a few things happened. I saw myself (in my mind's eye) putting my thumbs into the man's eyes and saying, "Be opened in the name of Jesus." And I knew beyond a shadow of a doubt that if I did that, it was going to happen.

Filled with this assurance, I kind of pushed Eddie out of the way (in love), and put my thumbs into those closed eyes and commanded them be opened in the name of Jesus. As quickly as the assurance came, it left. What remained was a sinking feeling and an "Oh no. What have I just done?" feeling. But we were trained, as part of the process of healing the sick, to ask the person what, if anything, was happening. So we did.

The blind man opened his eyes and said, "I can see your faces." We all wept as we continued to pray and interview, pray and interview. "I can see the man on the stage." Then, "I can see the people in the balcony." This took maybe 15 or 20 minutes, and we were still praying when Eddie and I looked at each other and said, "he's not saved!" That was kind of a shock, but as John used to say, it's very easy for someone to accept Jesus, after Jesus has just healed them. Eddie led him in the sinner's prayer and it was glorious to watch that formerly blind man with his eyes wide open and seeing, lift up his hands with great gratitude and receive his Savior."

Marti got "hooked on healing" and has been effectively praying for the sick ever since, as did most veterans of ministry team trips.

The concept of ministry team was born out of the spiritual genius of John Wimber, which was, undoubtedly, heavily influenced by Jesus' model of having a team of Twelve and then sending out a bigger team of seventy. Paul's missionary collaborations solidified the concept. Ministry teams fit marvelously into John's calling to equip the saints for the work of the church.

The inclusion of team members to pray for people at the conclusion of John's messages decentralized the focus on him as the primary source of healing. It put feet on John's repeated statement, "Everyone gets to play." The individual participation of team members multiplied personal kingdom ministry to the multitude of conference attendees.

Teams traveling to local churches often imparted the seeds of Vineyard values. The result in all this was kingdom expansion, and we all felt dynamically part of it.

Of course, the "perks" of being on ministry teams were many. We all got to participate in a bigger world geographically, culturally and of course spiritually. I must say we enjoyed traveling to New York, London, Frankfurt and Johannesburg; places we may never have seen otherwise. That's not to say that exciting places like Anaheim, Bend, Ruidoso, and Detroit did not have a charm of their own.

Often staying in homes we got the feel of foreign places, eating new foods and learning a few phrases of another language. We met new friends and made relationships, some of which have endured to this day. But the biggest benefit was seeing firsthand the bigger church at large and how powerfully the kingdom of God was spreading all over the world.

In 1987, John led a Signs and Wonders Conference in Frankfurt, Germany. We fielded a team of ten from Mission Viejo Vineyard. As was the norm, all of us paid our own way. We understood that there was a cost to kingdom ministry, which was further experienced, as we were crunched into economy seats for the eleven hour direct flight from LA. Without Ambien at the time, it was often a sleepless, uncomfortable night spent contorted into a tiny, torturous seat. But at least we had the choice of chicken, beef or some reasonable substitute.

Culture shock was then shared by all as we passed the X-rated advertisements in the Frankfurt terminal. After a jet lagged first night, in a hotel cubicle, we ventured out to an historic "platz" for a lunch of German beer, and of course, the ubiquitous frankfurter. It was actually quite nice at our patio table under the warming sun. We smiled at each other and felt the camaraderie. For the next five days we made our way up to the stage in front of five thousand people to pray for the sick. We felt the warmth of the Holy Spirit moving. Wonderful.

Before we went to do our satellite conference in Nuremberg, we visited Heidelberg, and its beautiful medieval, gothic castle. There was a very formal restaurant on the grounds with white tablecloths and waiters in tuxes. Our team, dressed in jeans and sweatshirts, huddled around a table in the crowded room. Our waiter, stiff as a penguin, came to serve us.

We had an affable, large set (6'4" x 240 lb.) team member by the name of Mike. All during the meal he would hike himself up, sit on the back of his chair, tell a funny story and start laughing out loud. The waiter stuck up his nose and refused to continue service. Mike sat back down and we all sheepishly finished our meal. When flying back through London, we all got in trouble when Mike climbed up on his luggage cart and rode it like a bucking bronco down the escalator. For a moment I thought to myself, "The Ugly American," then began to laugh. "Yeah, but we are the ministry team!"

In Nuremberg, we had team lunches at the host Lutheran church. The most lovely pastor welcomed us to the bottles of warm beer stored under the large dining table. This was definitely a moment of new cultural experience! The first night we taught on healing to an elderly audience. not much happened. The second night we taught on spiritual gifts to a youth gathering. The Holy Spirit fell, tongues broke out, prophecies were spoken and healing prayers flowed. All that we had received we gave away. Ah, that's ministry team.

On the final evening in Nuremberg, the gray-haired folks returned. I taught on experiencing the Father's love and invited the congregation to stand to receive a blessing. I invited the Holy Spirit to come and rest upon everyone. After a while, one man in his seventies, began to cry, and then fell to his knees and soon was face down on the carpet. One by one, every man in the room fell in the same way. Then the women followed. I suddenly realized that everyone in this greying congregation had been touched by WWII and carried the painful loss of their fathers in their hearts. Abba Father was coming to heal their wounds. The team member to bend over the first fallen man, and embrace him with love, was big Mike. Both were overcome with emotion.

For the next ten years, teams from all over the country followed in the footsteps of John Wimber and other Vineyard leaders in bringing renewal to the church. They crisscrossed most of the world's major continents. I've never heard of a team braving Antarctica... yet.

In 2002, I retired from senior pastoring, speaking mostly at conferences that supplied their own ministry teams. But last month, after teaching at a men's conference, I found myself laying hands on, and praying for each of the seventy men there. Towards the end, with my arm drooping from exhaustion, I asked myself, "What am I doing? Where is my ministry team?". Suddenly, I missed them! I needed them! The old, American Express line popped into mind: "Don't leave home without it!" It was then that I decided I'm not going on the road anymore, anywhere, without them, without a team, without my Marti's and Mike's.

17

WAITING ON THE SPIRIT

It was a tense moment to say the least! Well over two thousand people sitting on the edge of their seats waiting. Waiting for something to happen. And there, stage-front behind the microphone, stood John Wimber silently perusing the room. Two minutes of silence. Then five more. It seemed like an eternity. Then the nervous sound of the rustling of syllabus pages and bodies shifting on auditorium seats. Silence can be very uncomfortable.

After all this was the first big night of a Signs and Wonders conference. Stuff should be happening! People had come from all over England to this conference in Harrowgate. So many in fact that it demanded an overflow venue. Worship was awesome. John had preached brilliantly. Ministry time had come. John introduced it by saying, "Let's wait on the Spirit." And wait we did.

At about the twelve minute mark the pressure of the moment became palpable and with it someone on the Vineyard team blurted out a prophetic word. It was a bit harsh saying that the Holy Spirit was here to minister but there was a lack of faith in the people and repentance was in order to get things moving. That prompted John's first words, "Dear friends, I apologize for that word. It was not from the Lord. Nothing is wrong here. We just need to wait."

Soon after, John shared a word I had heard him give before, "People we've all come a great way through many challenges to get here tonight. I believe the Lord wants us to get a good night's rest because tomorrow great things are going to happen." And they did.

Waiting on the Spirit. No one did it like John. Perhaps it is one of the most overlooked treasures in the legacy he left us. The ability to resist having to make something happen under the pressure of expectation. The result was incredible things happening beyond our wildest imaginations. What was discovered through waiting made the Vineyard unique. Where did John get this ability?

I often wondered if it had something to do with his Quaker background. A man by the name of Gunner Payne, a Quaker and member of the Friends Church in Yorba Linda, led John to the Lord. When I asked Carol Wimber if John's Quaker influence affected his ability to wait, here was her answer:

"Well, that is an interesting question...the Quaker connection. Gunner Payne was the primary influence in both of our lives. He was the most Quakerish man of anyone we knew in the sense of contemplative, and plain dressing, and quiet living out your life before God and waiting on him for directions...never in a hurry, always listening to the Holy Spirit."

The Quaker practices in public meetings certainly demonstrates a value for waiting:

"While all Quakers meet for worship to hear more clearly God's "still small voice" (I Kings 19:12), Friends in the unprogrammed tradition base our worship entirely on expectant waiting. We take the Psalmist's advice literally: "Be still and know that I am God" (Psalm 46:10).

Occasionally, during meeting for worship, someone is moved to speak out of the silence. Although Friends value spoken messages which come from the heart and are prompted by the Spirit of God, we also value the silence and find that expectant worship may bring profound leadings"[1]

The ability to be comfortable with silence while waiting on the Lord requires some contemplative skills. It takes some discipline to remain passive in the Lord's presence and wait for him to move. John had this skill, although he was not built to be a traditional contemplative spending lots of time alone "on the mountain." Carol tells a humorous illustration of this:

"John was concerned about the whole direction we were going(in the Vineyard) and he needed to hear from God. Knowing he was not a Holy Man he thought perhaps if he could get away by himself alone on a quiet mountain, he would fast and pray and wait on the Lord until the LORD made His directions for the future clear to John. He was very serious about this. So I bade him fair well and off he went. I didn't know for how long because he had warned me he would not be back until he heard from God... even if it was weeks!

That was in the morning and I knew he had water with him so he was not in danger of perishing as the days of fasting and waiting went on and on. (Because who knew how long before the Lord would speak). That was at 8:00 in the morning. At 7:30 that evening he called from a phone booth in a McDonalds in San Bernardino explaining that he couldn't find a vacant room anywhere on the mountain and he was cold and discouraged and had just finished three Big Macs. I tried not to laugh out loud but to be sympathetic and I told him to come home, that it would be fine and that we (my prayer friends and I) had been praying all day anyway."

My own first big lesson on waiting on the Spirit came in 1984. I was doing a associate healing conference representing Vineyard Ministries in Bend, Oregon. It was my first time out on my own. The venue had changed from a local Calvary Chapel and we were hosted by a pastor from another stream of ministry, one that was a bit more Pentecostal.

The host pastor introduced me as a "signs and wonders worker like John Wimber." I could feel the pressure for some spectacular results. So when ministry time came I did my best to wait like I had seen John do. After a few minutes things got tense. The pastor couldn't take it. He got up on stage and took the microphone out of my hands. I was so nervous I readily gave it up.

The pastor began calling people up to the stage he knew had chronic health issues. He then began to pray for them. I feebly laid my hands on them too. Not much happened. It turned out to be quite a dismal beginning. I hardly slept that night. However the next day at a leaders meeting I could see the Holy Spirit "resting" on the pastor. I went over and put my hand on his head and blessed what the Spirit was doing. Shockingly, the power of the Spirit literally drove him to the ground. He was changed in a moment. We became life-long friends.

That Sunday morning he sat in the front row with not much to say. He gave me lots of room to wait this time. As I waited I noticed that all the church children were sitting very properly in the front rows. As it turns out the church was a bit legalistic and the kids had well prescribed behavior boundaries. After a while I received a leading that what the adults were working so hard for, i.e. the Spirit's power, the kids were going to get for free. So I had all the kids stand, elementary though high school age, and come up on stage. Then I asked the parents and the pastor to observe them carefully. The Holy Spirit came on them and they melted in the outpouring of divine love and power. The teary-eyed parents rushed up to embrace them and the Spirit fell on them also. What a difference waiting can make.

Over the years I observed John, again and again, waiting on the Spirit, scanning the room with that "look" in his eye. I learned to mimic that "look" as I took a deep breath, put up my spiritual antenna to listen to the Lord, and focused my mind's eye to see what the Father was doing. Ministry took on the rhythm of waiting and working. A pattern of contemplation and kingdom. The pattern of the life of Jesus. Jesus began his day in classic contemplation.

Very early in the morning, while it was still dark, Jesus got up, left the house and went off to a solitary place, where he prayed. (Mark 1:35)

Jesus demonstrates the essentials of contemplation: solitude, silence and prayer. It is very possible that a major part of his prayer life was silently waiting to hear his Father's voice giving instructions for the day. From that contemplative start each morning he would proceed to a day of intense kingdom activity. He models the life of an active contemplative. It established a pattern for effective ministry. Waiting and working.

I have found that developing the skill of contemplative prayer has enhanced my ability to wait on the Spirit in ministry situations whether they be in church or on the streets. I'm older now, and in a different season of life. I do not have a lot of energy to attempt to make stuff happen but I am still committed to "doing the stuff." Waiting on the Spirit is more essential than ever.

As I write this chapter I am investing in my contemplative development. I am on a silent retreat at a Benedictine hermitage high up on a mountain overlooking the wild coastlands of Big Sur, California. I'm walking in the footsteps of John Wimber. Just without the Big Macs.

Footnote:
1. "Silent Worship and Quaker Values: An Introduction" by Marsha Holliday, www.quaker.org

18

WIMBERISMS

As the pastor completed his sermon point, he lowered his chin, raised his eyebrows and adjusted his reading glasses to the tip of his nose and said, "Hello!" A moment later upon reaching another fine point he repeated his actions but this time said, "Are you hearing me?" For a moment I thought I was listening to John Wimber. It wasn't... exactly. It was Lance Pittluck, pastor of the Anaheim Vineyard, a man whose spirit and style does resemble John. He had taken over John's pulpit after his death. Mentored by John for many years he had picked up some of his mannerisms along the way, some of what we might call "Wimberisms."

Wimberisms are short, often pithy, statements John made during his teaching and ministry. One of the most classic was, "The meat is in the street." In the early days the Vineyard was criticized for their emphasis on worship, especially intimate worship that focused on experiencing the presence of God. As worship times began to equal the time windows for preaching and teaching, critics said we were devaluing the Word. In doing so we weren't going deeper into the Word, into the real meat. To this John answered, "The meat is in the street." In other words, it was in obeying the Word and doing the kingdom works that one discovered the deeper meaning.

As I was writing this chapter Lance texted me another that he remembered well, "Everyone gets to play." These simple words capture the essence of ministry in the church. Everyone gets to exercise their gifts and talents and do the works that Jesus did. We all get to "Do the stuff." Another classic Wimberism.

While these and other Wimberisms echo through the public halls of Vineyard history, its the ones that I heard in private that had the most impact on me. Although their deepest application was found in unique personal situations, I believe that they can have universal benefit. As Henri Nouwen quoted, "What is most personal is most universal." With that in mind here are my top seven.

Believe it or not the most vivid phrase that immediately pops to mind is, "I hate hot!" These immortal words were spoken by John in a New York City Magic Pan restaurant. Magic Pan was once a well-known purveyor of French crepes. John, Carol, Janet and I had finished the main course and ordered dessert crepes. Janet remembers ordering Cherries Jubilee and John ordering Bananas Foster. Janet's crepe was served with dark cherries and liqueur sauce cooled over a mountain of vanilla ice cream. John's came out in flames as the server ignited the alcohol poured over the bananas drenched with a butter, cinnamon, and dark rum sauce. You could see the fire reflected in his eyes as he proclaimed, "I hate hot!" Janet and he quickly exchanged desserts.

Those words, while devoid of any deeper spiritual meaning, however, speak volumes to me about Classic Vineyard lifestyle. They remind me of the intimate, relational exchanges that occurred around sharing a meal together. So often, it was around a table, we got to really know each other.

It was on that same New York trip in the early 80's that my number two personal Wimberism was born. For most of our ministry years Janet and I lived with a philosophy of pursuing spartan living. On a limited income, luxury was not in our field of vision. It came into it when John reached over from the seat in back of us on the plane and offered us some very nice Swiss chocolate. Our eyes grew wider when a limousine dropped us off in front of the Essex House Hotel on Central Park. With that as our base of exploring the city, we enjoyed breakfast at the Plaza and dinner at Mamma Leone's. Janet and I would pinch each other and say, "Is this for real?"

Reality hit us a couple days later when a dented Yellow Cab dropped us off in front of a weathered Holiday Inn on Staten Island. Walking to our room on the dingy, faded carpet we passed room service trays that had been sitting in the hallway for a while. The pungent odor of fermenting thousand island dressing was a bit disconcerting. John, sensing my alarm, turned to me and said, "Eddie, I have taught you how to 'abound' and now I'm teaching you how to 'abase.' " The words and the lesson stuck, " Abase and abound." Every time we are led down a hallway to another cave-like hotel room I look at Janet and say, "Looks like we're about to 'abase' ...'abound' must be just around the corner."

Number three came out of similar situations spending time with John and Carol. Whenever the Vineyard wagon hit a bump in the road and a few people were tossed off for one reason or another, John would look at Carol and say, "It's just you and me babe!" So true. In the end its all about your marriage, family and a few good friends. I can't tell you how many times Janet and I have gone for a walk after a "bump" in our kingdom journey and repeated these words to each other. In fact, we have a favorite greeting card we have exchanged on several anniversaries that shows a couple together on a roller coaster, coming over the top and headed down the steep incline, their hands gripping the bar, their eyes are enlarged with trepidation. The line on the card says, "Here we go again!" Inside it should read, "It's just you and me babe!"

Once the bump we hit was in our own marriage. It was the kind where you both get tossed, feel injured by the other and get overly focused on your own well-being. Working through the wrinkles in marriage can be a lot of work. It was when I complained to John about the work I was putting into the process that he had these words. Number four: "Eddie, you need to forget about yourself and be a friend to your wife." A personal Wimberism that cut to the quick! A mantra for marriage that I have never forgotten. One that I would need to hear again, and act upon, whenever I would get too full of myself.

Months later, Janet and I had another dinner with John and Carol. After dinner, John and I were walking along the bayshore on Balboa Island. Full after a great meal and feeling good about life, I asked John an all too revealing question. I said, "John. what do you think I'll get out of this?" Indicating that there must be some kind of big reward for courageously working through our marriage issues. A bigger church? Bigger ministry? This birthed a sobering number five, "You get more of Jesus. Isn't that enough for you?" Enough said.

As you can see not all personal Wimberisms were as fun as "I hate hot!" And after twelve years of hanging around John you would think I didn't need the less humorous ones but by 1993 I was ready for another one. That year I was honored to speak at the International Pastor's Conference held in Anaheim. I had been doing a lot of conferences in the Vineyard on the subject of the Father's love. For this conference I was asked to speak on Spiritual Fathering - the effects of the Father's love on leadership.

Feeling that I had a prophetic gift to bring this message to the world, and now to the Vineyard leadership, I began to prepare. I think I got myself too revved up in wanting to convince everyone of the importance of spiritual fathering. In any case I sort of overdid it. I spoke a little too long. Maybe a little too loud. I felt bad when John, who was not in the best of health, had to leave before I was done. The Holy Spirit was gracious and ministered to many. However, I was despondent.

Weeks later, back at the restaurant in Newport Beach, I had another walk with John after dinner. I told him that I was sorry about my message at the conference. I knew that I had become parental in my delivery. I had become the expert trying to convince others of the importance of my discoveries about the Father. John excepted my apology and then said, "We are all just beggars giving away to others the bread we have received." Number six. O Lord, please help me remember that one.

The last one, number seven, is fitting to end with. After many years went by, with battles won and battles lost, Janet asked John, "Does it ever get easier?" John was quick to answer, "O yes! All at once it will get really easy!" There was a twinkle in his eye.

Lance texted me again today. Another Wimberism had come to mind: "Service what you sell!" That's a good one. Perhaps you remember it and others that I did not mention. Perhaps you have a personal one all of your own. Perhaps this is the first you have heard of them. In any case, may they resonate in your life. May the wisdom and love hidden inside them be a blessing to you. Everyone of them has been a gift from my Father to me.

EPILOGUE

I remember sitting around a table encircled with white plastic chairs. The room was set up for 150 people to have dinner. There were only 50 there. A disappointing turnout.

At our table was my wife Janet, Ed and Jill McGlasson and John Wimber. It was about a year before John went home to be with the Lord, and the ravages of a stroke and cancer had taken their toll on John's body. He was quite thin, skin pale, and having to spray a liquid to lubricate his mouth to speak. However his eyes still sparkled with a transcendent light.

This evening was being held to promote John's attempt to launch a new radio ministry - something I never sensed his heart was really into. Nevertheless, he was giving it a shot. I wondered how he would negotiate his speaking and ministry to such a small group. After all I had seen him hit the ball "out of the park" in front of multiple thousands time and time again.

As usual, he was front and center during worship, hands lifted in praise. With some extra effort he rose and took his place beside the pulpit, a black music stand. And then he preached an eloquent message on Jesus' kingdom ministry. In conclusion he waited on the Spirit until he received a few words of knowledge for people who needed healing. As his ministry team we came forward to help John pray for the sick.

In Carol's book, John Wimber: The Way it Was, she tells how John remembered that evening:

"I remembered the night of the fundraiser and how happy he was when he came home. ' Oh, Carol, it was so wonderful! I was tired and I had a hard time hearing but the Lord was there. He healed a lady and…' I interrupted him to ask how many had come. 'Oh, not many, probably fifty or so - and I felt bad for the hosts - but it was such a great night - the Lord touched almost everybody. Thank you, Jesus!'

Whether in front of 50 or 5,000 John's ministry always contained the "original formula." It was always Classic Vineyard. Watching John that night, knowing what he was physically going through, and seeing the authenticity of his life and commitment to Jesus and kingdom ministry, I knew that's how I wanted to live the rest of my life. I wanted to live with that same excitement, the same commitment to the message and call at the end of my ministry as I had at the beginning. I wanted to "Live Like John."

In the Fall of 1997 John was hospitalized again. I went to visit him. Entering his room, I was greeted by John's son Tim. As we both stood along side his bed, he stirred from his sleep and looked up and said, "Well, look at this. Two of my sons are here. One of my natural sons and one of my spiritual sons." We drew near and he blessed us both.

Shortly after that, on November 17th I received a call that John was passing away as a result of a fall causing a massive hemorrhage. I rushed to the hospital, reaching his room where many family and friends had gathered. After a while people began to filter out. There was a moment when John lay at rest in an empty room. I quietly entered and stood at his bedside. I wept silently. I bent over and kissed his forehead saying good-by. I felt his presence.

Standing there in the silence a thought came to me. John is leaving a legacy for us to walk in. There is a mantle of anointing to be passed on. I said to myself, if there is, then certainly I would say yes to receiving a portion of it. So I reached and took ahold of John's hand and prayed, "Lord, if John is leaving a legacy, passing on a mantle, I will take it. Yes Lord I will take it."

It has been nearly twenty years since that day and John's legacy lives on in the Vineyard and other streams of ministry that encircle the globe. Multiple men and women have picked up their portion of the mantle. As a result, the kingdom has expanded exponentially through a myriad of creative worship forms, a multitude of teachers and preachers exploring every nuance of the kingdom and a mighty army of everyday signs and wonder workers.

For those of us that would call our tribe "Vineyard," we certainly have a delightful inheritance. It is my hope that in this collection of stories you have once again tasted that original formula and have been refreshed by Classic Vineyard.

Eddie Piorek pastored the Mission Viejo Vineyard for over twenty years. He is the author of The Father Loves You, The Central Event and other books. He lives with his wife Janet in San Clemente, California.

Printed in Great Britain
by Amazon

24166779R00094